Dancing to the Concertina's Tune

Dancing
to the
Concertina's
Tune

A Prison Teacher's
Memoir

Tune

by Jan Walker

Northeastern University Press – Boston

Northeastern University Press

Copyright 2004 by Janet D. Walker

Library of Congress Cataloging-in-Publication Data
Walker, Jan (Janet D.)
Dancing to the concertina's tune : a prison teacher's memoir /
by Jan Walker.
p.   cm.
ISBN 1-55553-601-8 (pbk. : alk. paper) —
ISBN 1-55553-602-6 (cloth : alk. paper)
1. Walker, Jan (Janet D.) 2. Prison educators—Washington
(State)—Biography. 3. McNeil Island Penitentiary. I. Title.
HV8883.3.U52W35   2004
365'.66—dc22   2004001101

Designed by Lindsay Himes

Composed in Electra by Coghill Composition Company, Richmond,
Virginia. Printed and bound by Edwards Brothers, Inc., Lillington, North
Carolina. The paper is EB Natural, an acid-free stock.

MANUFACTURED IN THE UNITED STATES OF AMERICA
08   07   06   05   04   5   4   3   2   1

To correctional educators and inmate students

Education opens locked doors

Contents

Preface

In 2001, nearly two million people were incarcerated in prison or jail, according to the United States Department of Justice (www .ojp.usdoj.gov/bjs/crimoff.htm) More than four million others were on probation or parole. The Bureau of Justice projects that one of every twenty persons in the United States will serve time in prison. If current trends continue, that will include 28 percent of black males, 16 percent of Hispanic males, and 4.4 percent of white males.

As prison populations grow and prison costs increase, funds for offender programs, including education, decrease. More than 95 percent of all offenders are released. Each year some six hundred thousand of them return to our communities, many of them with the same education and skills they had at the time of their arrest.

You'll meet some convicted offenders in this book. I hope my story increases your understanding of prisons and inmates. I hope you become a supporter of correctional education.

Acknowledgments

Thanks to all the members of my family who have listened to my stories and frustrations since 1979; to Eve Begley Kiehm, who did the first edit; to writers' group members Colleen and Frank Slater, Kathryn Arnold, Kathleen O'Brien, and Suzanne Hilton for their suggestions; to my daughter Marla Klipper and my sister Joyce Olsen for their careful reading and comments; to retired Department of Corrections health care manager Ginny Hull for the final read; to all the teachers and prison staff who supported my work; and to inmate students who chose to learn and change.

Special thanks to Alice Payne, Tom Rabak, and Gil Burton for my early years at McNeil Island Corrections Center, to the entire team of the program we called Project Social Responsibility, and to editor Sarah E. Rowley for her advice.

Introduction:
Preview of an Unusual Career

I taught adult felons for eighteen years—women and men who had murdered; raped; assaulted; pillaged; bought, sold, and used drugs; and committed unimaginable offenses against those they purported to love. No matter their crime, I met them as students and treated them as such. I believe even those who came seeking a mother's ear, or perhaps a priest's, found information that helped them think, wisdom that helped them learn, and antics that helped them remember.

I cut my correctional education teeth at Washington state's women's prison teaching traditional home economics, family dynamics, parenting skills, and related subjects meant to help women reconnect with their families. During the early years, I tailored standard college courses and educational materials to the population and devoted off-hours to research and curriculum development. In time some of my work was published, and other correctional educators put it to use. After eleven years I transferred from the women's prison to McNeil Island Corrections Center, a medium-custody men's facility, to introduce parenting and family courses and to coordinate an orientation program.

Much of this book is about my experiences with male offenders, but women's stories are here too, and tales of gender differences. Female teachers could hug a sobbing female inmate who'd gotten bad news from home and needed a steady shoulder, but sobbing males (and there were many) had to be kept at a distance. Rather than a shoulder, I offered a roll of toilet paper procured from janitorial supplies. Boxed tissues would have been nicer, but those carried inside from home disappeared within hours, box and all.

Prison is a unique society with absolute rules beyond those legislated by state or federal governments. Through the final decades of the twentieth century, barred cell blocks gave way to electronically controlled living units. The old convict code declined, and a new code slipped in, almost unnoticed, to take its place. It has to do with the unequivocal segregation of prisons and communities; it is symbolized by double rows of high chain-link fences topped with rigid, spiraled razor wire. The wire, named concertina, is meant to shred flesh to ribbons. None enter or leave a prison's confines without permission. All are locked in during their stay. All who go inside, in any capacity, dance to the concertina's tune.

1 Going Inside the Prison Fence

When sun shines on Puget Sound, her surface shimmers like se-
quins on a ballroom gown and makes waterfront real estate prices
seem almost reasonable. Most land along the sound's mainland
and multi-island shores is privately owned. Some small plats be-
long to Indian nations whose ancestors once used its plenty, some
to the federal government for shipyards and military use, some to
the state for public recreation. One island in the South Sound,
named McNeil for a Hudson's Bay steamship captain, belongs en-
tirely to the state. Two-thirds of its 4,400 acres are forested, a pristine wildlife refuge. One-third is a medium-custody correctional
facility, the last operating prison in North America accessible only
by boat.

   In 1977, when I first visited McNeil Island, the prison compound was a century-old federal penitentiary, an ugly scar at the
forest's edge. Dirty yellow and noncolor buildings with dingy
barred windows stood on a hill above the dock where passenger
ferries came and went twenty-four hours a day, carrying prison
employees, inmates, and authorized visitors. Before going inside
the fence, I looked east across the sound to the sleepy town of
Steilacoom and the mainland dock where corrections officers
check passengers' credentials. Freedom was a twenty-minute boat

ride away. Snow-clad Mount Rainier, skirted with thick stands of fir, cedar, and hemlock, loomed above the town and sound. At sunset on sunny days, the mountain blushes pink for a time, then disappears into darkness.

How, I wondered, did men housed inside the fence cope with the incongruity of nature's beauty and prison's anguish?

I was on the island as a visitor with students from my Tacoma Community College Family Relationships class, most of whom startled a bit when the prison gate closed behind us. One of my students worked in the prison as a correctional officer and acted as our guide. He'd heard about the class, or perhaps my teaching style, and believed it would help him in his daily interactions with inmates. I'd never before met anyone who worked in prison, never known anyone sentenced to do time, never given prison or inmates, or their interactions, much thought. That made me a rather typical American.

Another officer joined us in the wide, high-ceilinged corridor, and off we went into the dismal, almost dead interior of the old cell house. We were subdued, reverent even, but our hard-soled shoes announced our presence as we climbed steel-mesh stairs and walked cell-block tiers. We glanced into cells that were bedrooms, bathrooms, living rooms, and sometimes kitchens for men clever enough to rig electric wires to simple pieces of metal—perhaps a contraband fork—to cook stolen meat. (Plastic utensils have since replaced metal ones in most prisons.) Their crowded, dank cells, built for five men, had been double-bunked and housed ten by then, and they reeked of overused toilets, under-washed bodies, and despair.

Somewhere, on one of those tiers, we viewed what my student called the *lala cells*. Lalas trade sexual favors for food or other commodities from the prison store, or art items created by inmates for sale and trade. Such men are generally called punks or any number of slang terms for their sexual role, but they will remain lalas in my mind. Though my student guide had prepared me for meeting them, I felt uncomfortable. We were looking into cells that were their homes, and into a world of gender roles unfamiliar to me. The lalas were playing cards; at the very least, we were intruding in their card game. Other cards, presumably from a worn deck, served as makeshift hair rollers, preparation for their late-night dates. Some lalas wore lipstick, blush, eye shadow. They were accustomed to visitors walking by, and they paid us little heed even when our guide said the Avon representative who sold them their cosmetics often achieved top-sales recognition in her region.

The prison administration obviously honored their gender roles by permitting such sales inside the fence. In fact, makeup bothered me less than the sight of adults sitting around playing cards during what I considered the work hours of the day. I had no understanding then of what "doing time" meant, or how few jobs were available inside the prison fence.

From the cell house we went to prison industries, to me a much more appealing place. Daylight filtered through fly- and dust-specked windows. Men worked at physical tasks: welding, electronic repair, furniture making. My dad, a carpenter by profession, had been adept in many crafts. As firstborn in a family of girls, I had a special bond with my father, a typical birth-order characteristic. Dad taught me to see the artisan in all work. Those men, working with their hands to create or restore useful items, gave me an odd sense of all being well in spite of the setting.

Those prison workrooms were male places, with Marilyn Monroe pinups, machine noise, and torch flames. Men wore safety goggles, work gloves, sturdy clothing, and boots. I felt less uncomfortable there than I had in the cell house, but I was still out of my realm. Over the years I taught in prison, I heard numerous inmates say visitors walking past their cells and classrooms made them feel like they were monkeys in a zoo.

I now know only a handful of incarcerated adults ever get hired for prison industry jobs. Those who do are generally long-termers whose money goes home to support a family. They have their own inside fraternity and shun any they consider homosexual.

We made the rounds—the prison hospital and chapel, an open barracks–like living unit for those who'd climbed the privilege ladder, the mess hall, staff dining room, mail room, administrative offices. We heard stories of some famous men who'd done time there: gangster Mickey Cohen for tax evasion; Teamster president Dave Beck, convicted of racketeering; auto thief Charles Manson, who later was convicted of the heinous Tate–La Bianca murders. An officer dangling chains from his hands told us about a man soon to be famous, at least inside the federal system, for information he had revealed in an attempt to lighten his sentence. The body chains were meant for him, for his transport across the sound, where he would be met by federal officials and flown to another institution.

"He's wearing a snitch jacket," the officer rattling the chains said. "Nowhere's safe for him now, and he knows it. Snitches make their own death row."

The male students in our tour group asked pointed questions about the move, including how many guards would accompany the prisoner into an airplane lavatory, and whether the cuffs would be removed while he urinated. The question reminded me I needed to use a restroom before we boarded the boat for the twenty-minute crossing to Steilacoom and our parked cars. I was reading door signs when one man asked if the officer would demonstrate the body chains on me. Without my agreeing to what my students considered a great laugh, the officer cuffed my wrists, snapped a chain around my waist, and knelt to put ankle bracelets in place.

I remember a chill swept over me, and my stomach churned. Did I gasp for breath before the chill gave way to heat so intense it felt as if I stood in flames? I had the odd feeling my hair had caught fire. The officer must have seen alarm in my look or felt it radiating from me. "You claustrophobic?" he asked.

I hadn't considered myself so, but I seemed to be in the throes of a panic attack. "Take them off. Get me out of them." My need for the restroom escalated to near-emergency. "Just get the damn things off."

"Key's lost," someone joked.

But it wasn't funny, not to me. It felt as though my essence, my spirit, had disappeared. My students' chatter, once we were outside the fence, seemed removed from me, like the noise of a radio in another room. The ferry approached, seagulls called, a blue heron waded in the shallows. Mount Rainier loomed. All was well in my world, but the lost feeling lingered. The memory lingers still. Perhaps it served a purpose, though I didn't know then I would teach inside the prison fence, eventually on the island, or how many times I'd see men—and occasionally women—in body chains. Hundreds of men and several women told me they had experienced emotions similar to mine. It goes far beyond the humiliation of being handcuffed, which is bad enough, they say. It's worse than the finality of prison: it's the loss of self.

Body chains—shackles—serve their purpose in just that way. Officials responsible for transporting prisoners need them to be subdued for reasons of safety—the officials', the public's, the prisoners'. It is an officer's duty and obligation to manage prisoners with dignity, but dignity takes a backseat to public safety every time. Even pregnant women must endure cuffs and chains, though most jurisdictions now cuff their hands in front of their bodies as added protection should they trip and fall forward.

My moment in shackles underscored a valuable lesson my mother lived by and taught: look at the person, not the chains. (She said look inside the person, or some such, but the message remains the same.) Her teachings, and Dad's, followed me through life and quite possibly prepared me for my unusual career as a correctional educator, and my return to McNeil Island thirteen years later.

2 Behind the Badge

Two years after my brief introduction to life inside the fence, community colleges by legislative mandate became education providers inside all Washington state prisons, and my department head asked me to move from the main Tacoma Community College campus to the women's prison near Gig Harbor to set up a Home and Family Life program.

"One year," I said. "I'll go out there for one year."

For the next seventeen years, I agreed to one more year. Even now, it seems an odd career for one who proclaimed aloud from second grade through college and beyond, "I will never teach." My declaration began when my second grade teacher died suddenly, and my mother, who'd retired from teaching to rear a family, stepped in to complete the year. Until then, because of myopia, I had a favored place beside the teacher's desk. Mom got me glasses; moved me, desk and all, to the spot dictated by alphabet; and taught me more by her principles than primers. Through the ensuing years, I watched her prepare lessons and grade papers and listened to her fret about struggling students. Under her tutelage I achieved an acceptable level of tolerance for human differences, and a certainty I would never develop the patience necessary to teach. Most teachers, it seemed, spent inordinate time with students on the low end of the learning curve.

I now admit my first two post-college positions, one as a county extension agent, one as a nutrition consultant for the Dairy Council, involved teaching; they provided ideal experience and credentials to become a community college instructor. In truth, I first became a teacher at age fourteen, when I took over leadership of a group of nine- and ten-year-old boys barred by sex from a girls' 4-H cooking and sewing club. That must have required patience, but I recall it as fun, not work at all. Those boys hand-hemmed tea towels and mixed muffin batter just enough to blend ingredients without incorporating too much air. I picture them with stained T-shirts and grubby hands.

My mother, whose path I long tried to avoid, would say that wasn't true: they always washed their hands. She often accused me of exaggeration and overdramatization of simple life events. I wish she'd lived long enough to know how well both served me, especially in prison classrooms. As teacher/author Gail Godwin said, "Good teaching is one-fourth preparation and three-fourths pure theater." I made every classroom my private stage and played whatever role my students needed each hour, each day, for each subject.

Prison classrooms aren't remarkable: they have student and teacher desks or tables, blackboards (or white acetate boards), bookshelves, file cabinets, pencil sharpeners, and windows that need washing. Rather, it's the students who are notable for the circuitous routes they travel to arrive at a place called correctional education. For all the time I spent with them, their world inside remains foreign to me. I never stayed the night in prison, and that makes all the difference.

Still, something I brought to my work fit their needs: something more than a college degree and prior experience. Skills and passions honed in my family of origin and carried forth with my children followed me to my correctional educator role. I taught my beliefs: all behaviors have consequences; proper discipline

teaches; and children deserve love and care and accurate information about their family history.

Washington state's women's prison, when I first went there in
1979, seemed pleasant when compared to the old penitentiary I'd
visited two years before. Single-story redbrick buildings and a spa-
cious cement courtyard were softened by lawns, flowering trees,
shrubs, and flowers. Women wore clothing they brought from
home; most moved about freely, gathering in groups to talk,
stretching out on a patch of grass to enjoy the sun. To an untrained
eye, the whole looked like a private college campus, and it made
much of our new-employee training seem ill suited.

We were fingerprinted; photographed; told a prison riot was a
matter of when, not if; and cautioned at every turn. We watched
a video that included footage on searching a toilet for contraband,
and heard about an officer whose fingers, or parts of them, were
blown off by a retractable pen/bomb. We were told a male former
art teacher had worn a rubber apron to prevent groping by aggressive inmates.

We met our students, who'd been sent to the prison (then
called Purdy Treatment Center for Women) to get the help they
needed; well over half of them had been convicted of property
crimes. Our classes certainly qualified as help, though it's not clear
who learned the most, students or teachers. We all found women
enrolled in our classes who could have been our mothers, sisters,
daughters, neighbors, or friends. Some of their stories boggled our
minds. A young mother in my first parenting classes had been
sixteen and pregnant at the time of her arrest. A judge issued an
order to chain her to the hospital birthing table so she wouldn't
escape during delivery.

I went inside to teach female prisoners and found humanity in
a microcosm. Two professional colleagues who moved from other
positions to McNeil Island Corrections Center (MICC) when it
became a state facility said I'd find the same thing with men, and
an even greater need for my work. They arranged for me to teach
an experimental parenting class at the island for one quarter as a

guest from the women's prison. They were right: the men needed parenting and family and personal responsibility courses too.

My official transfer to MICC meant going through the mug shot/fingerprinting/badge-making routine of prison employment again. The Department of Corrections (DOC) officer who took my photo and typed vital information on the back of my MICC badge looked at my official title—a lengthy one—and at my request settled on "parenting teacher." He typed away on his IBM Selectric and misspelled parenting as "parienting." He shrugged when I pointed out the typo, looked at me, shook his head.

"Parenting teacher. For a bunch of screwed-up cons. Locking 'em up's best thing ever happened to their kids."

He needn't have spoken: he projected his disdain, and he wasn't alone. Though prison administrators know positive family connections increase an inmate's chances of successful reintegration into society, not all line staff buy it. He shoved the badge in a plastic sleeve, laminated it, punched a hole in the top, inserted a clip, and handed it to me. For the last seven years of my career, I wore a badge that proclaimed me the *parienting* teacher.

Whatever my label, all who met me knew I taught, counseled, and advised in the context of personal and social responsibility. I wanted McNeil Island inmates to reconsider their choices, their lives, their families and communities, and their own personhood. I wanted to be more than just another authority figure dishing out information or rules to inmates.

They had already been appraised, found guilty, sentenced, and incarcerated. I didn't serve as judge, jury, or jailer. My goal was to precipitate change. That kept me going through political and philosophical turmoil in the prison system; moments of despair and doubt when I dealt with someone whose crime I found particularly deplorable; and occasional encounters with taxpayers who berated me for wasting public monies to teach scumbags, street rats, human garbage. More than once I wiped another's spittle from my face. Taxpayers irate at the costs of crime, in my experience, delivered their views with overabundant saliva, and in one case a deliberate wad of unpleasant bodily fluid.

I agree with them about the expense, more than thirty billion dollars a year nationwide to operate existing prisons, build new ones, and settle lawsuits when paroled felons reoffend. As those costs climb, the dollars spent on inmate education, job-skill training, and chemical dependency and mental health treatment sharply decline. Is that what taxpayers want, I wonder, or what we get when we vote for politicians who promise to be tough on crime?

Over the years I have also met numerous people who asked intelligent questions about my experience and expressed concern for the men and women inside. Recently someone thanked me. She's a new acquaintance, and I must confess I looked at her to be certain it wasn't a snide comment, though I'd already seen in her a person of truth and depth. "Thank you for doing that job," she said. "It's so needed."

There it is, the other reason I stayed for eighteen years. Someone needed to do it, and I did it quite well. Only one question remains in my mind: Did it matter?

3 The Parenting Experiment

Through the 1980s, only a few correctional educators across the country offered parenting and family classes to incarcerated dads, a fact I saw as a commentary on the American family and where we were in our sociological development. The men who became my students in an experimental parenting class at MICC saw it as "effed up."

Pierce College, the education provider at MICC, signed off on a basic two-credit course one night a week for the eleven-week summer quarter.

In summer, men are allowed to stay outdoors until nine o'clock recall for count. Yard time is prized for fresh air and exercise and the opportunity to talk without being overheard—no small thing in prison.

They did enroll, the maximum twenty-five, all interested in the material or curious about the instructor. If a couple of them hoped I'd carry messages back to the women's prison, where I taught days, they abandoned the notion in the first few minutes.

"Do you know Jane . . . Audrey . . . Connie . . . ?"

I shook my head.

Descriptions followed. I kept shaking my head and tried to stop the grin tugging at my face muscles. I'd advised those women not to play dress-up and spend their photo chits on Polaroids for male inmate pen pals they found through an incarcerated friend.

"Do you know what they do with those pictures?" I asked those women. "Do you want to be some inmate's fantasy? You can do better."

"She thinks they use our pictures to jerk off," one woman said.

"So?" said another. Some women didn't care. They were looking for attention, someone who could write a stimulating letter; and who could blame them? Days are long and nights lonely in prison. They bought photo chits, a dollar per photo in those days; fussed with hair and makeup; and did things with their clothes to make them look good, sexy. I'd seen dozens of such pictures before they were sent off.

Now I looked at twenty-five men, all dressed in khaki, all clean and combed. Nice-looking men, not much older than my sons. When they entered the classroom and took seats, they became my students, and I'd treat them with the same concern and respect I gave the women.

"No," I told those men, "I don't know any of those women."

One man snorted. "She knows them, but she's too smart to give anything up."

I walked to where he sat, dead center in the room. He'd been slumped in his seat, eyes down, when I took attendance, but he sat straight now. He had light brown hair, sad brown eyes, and little resemblance to his badge photo. "You're right," I said, "personal information remains private. I don't carry their names to the streets, as they say, and I won't abuse yours either."

He smiled, and some sadness left his eyes. Ted (all inmate names have been changed for their privacy) enrolled in the class because something troubled him, and he hoped I could help. I have a knack for reading need in faces and posture, in simple gestures and words. Those men were all there for a reason, but some hurt more than others.

We met in an ugly old classroom (there's now a modern Inmate Services Building) with battered chair desks, a blackboard still dusty from haphazard erasing, evening sun baking dirt on windows that didn't open enough to air out cigarette smoke. Stained acoustical tiles drooped from the ceiling; faded institution-yellow paint covered the walls, except where plaster chunks had chipped off. A scarred and bulky instructor's desk, gunmetal grey, stood front and center. I pushed against it with hip and thigh to get it out of my way. Men jumped to help and shoved it into a far corner. Testosterone and male chivalry, I learned, often worked to a female teacher's benefit.

I wove through the narrow spaces created by those chair desks lined up in rows, five across, five deep, and cramped. "Spread out if you like. I'm going to wander around and get acquainted, put names with faces. Tell me about your children. Gender, ages. No names unless you choose. I know it's risky to say too much inside."

The air in the room changed as men relaxed. We spent the first hour in informal discussions of children and course content. By period movement at seven o'clock, I had a good sense of their needs and could begin to do my work on patterns in families. During the ten-minute break I wrote on the dusty chalkboard, "About 75 percent of our parenting methods are those we unconsciously adopted from our parents or caregivers." Those who hadn't left the room for break watched me. Some itched to get their hands on the photocopied materials I'd stacked on the shoved-aside teacher's desk, but they waited. They were more polite and patient than most of my women students, but that may have been because we were on trial in a sense. They would determine whether parenting and family classes would be added to the education schedule.

After break I distributed the photocopied material that would serve as their text, along with a syllabus and notebook paper. Precious notebook paper, carefully guarded by education office staff. (I tended to give out far more paper than authorized and supplemented the supplies with my own when necessary, knowing a certain amount would be used for nonschool purposes such as writing letters to incarcerated women.)

We looked through the material, which was traditional positive-parenting information I'd adapted from texts written for parents who lived with their children. I packaged it in ten chapters or units to fit the ten-week study/one-week final format the community college followed.

I explained that Positive Parenting was a lecture/discussion course and told them that the more they discussed, the less I lectured, and that the ten assignments, one due each week, were homework, not to be completed during class time.

Much of the education program at MICC was of necessity self-paced in a learning lab environment. A night class in which everyone worked on the same topic at the same time, exchanged opinions and stories, talked out loud, and even laughed was a departure from the norm. The men thrived on the format. (In the years after my departure, lecture classes were increasingly eliminated, replaced by self-paced education, in an attempt to reduce education costs.)

We went over the course syllabus. One man said, "You serious? Twenty-five percent of the grade's based on class participation?"

"Absolutely. That's as much as Pierce College would permit. This is a college course, so they get to call some shots. I hope it's one of the most important life courses you ever take. It's about your children." I returned to the board, pointed at the statement there. "It's about what *you* can do to change any negative parenting behaviors you picked up from those who reared you so *your* children don't use them when they're parents."

It's almost frightening how much an experienced teacher senses in her students. I could see all of them remembered unpleasant moments in their childhoods, and how they felt years later when they'd done the same thing to a child in their care. I spoke of something from my own experience. Self-disclosure, so important in teaching parenting and family classes, was imperative with this group. There was a strong possibility I'd been oversold to them. We needed common ground on which to connect as adults equal in humanity though distanced in so many other ways.

"We're not here to blame our parents for what we've become," I said. "We're here to learn about positive parenting. I believe parents do the best they can in their given circumstances. It's a difficult task most of us undertake without any formal training. We're here to remedy that."

Twenty-five men nodded. Ted was the first to trust me enough to disclose his personal struggles as a dad in prison. He spoke with pride and love of his two sons. Then his face changed, his chin dropped, and he slid down in his seat.

"Their mother changed their last name. She let some asshole move in with her. Told the boys he's their new dad, I'm a convict."

"Were you ever married to their mother?" I'd grown accustomed to marriage as the rare exception over the years I'd taught incarcerated women.

"Still am," Ted said. "She wants a divorce, but she's waiting until I get out so I can pay for it. Says the guy's adopting the boys."

The man in front of Ted turned around. "She's your legal old lady and she's got some other dude living with her? That's cold, man."

"Living with her, calling my boys his, living on support I send through my mom. I always supported my kids, I got money set aside, my mom helps some."

And so began the discussion part of the course, which veered from basic positive parenting skills to legalities. By then I had some fame in correctional education as the author of a nontraditional parenting book, *Parenting from a Distance: Your Rights and Responsibilities*, which focuses especially on issues of incarcerated parents. But that wasn't the course Pierce College approved, and it was not what I'd contracted to teach.

I concluded neither Ted nor his wife understood much about family law. Ted slumped deeper. "She's their mother, she takes care of them and all, she needs the money. It's not about the money; it's about my name."

The room went quiet. The men watched to see how I'd react. Would I shrug it off as many in the system did? Inmates often heard, "Sounds like a personal problem to me," or "Shoulda thought of that before you did the crime."

I went into lecture mode. Or perhaps I preached—a fault, I

confess. "First, unless your parental rights have been legally terminated, your sons cannot be adopted." Ted's eyes showed he knew
that at some level, but fear blurs awareness. "Second, most schools
require children's birth certificates to enroll them and use the last
name on their birth certificate, though teachers will sometimes
bend to a parent's request."

Ted sat up a little. "I'm on their birth certificate. I was there
when they were born." A hint of smile touched his sad brown eyes.
"Doctor let me catch the younger one."

Such first-touch bonding is considered powerful, a strong de-
terrent to future child abuse, a strong tie for parents of the child.
What had happened between Ted and his wife? Was she using the
children as pawns now for her own gain? Rather than ask in class,
I went with what I knew.

"You have several positives going for you. If you don't have a
court order preventing you from contacting the children, you can
check with the school about the names they're using. If you
do . . ."

A man at the back of the room growled, "Oh, yeah, sure, he
can just call them up, say 'Hey, Dude, what name my kids go by?'"
All calls from Washington state prison inmates are made collect,
and the recipient is advised the caller is in prison.

"I don't have any orders against me," Ted said. "I never hurt
those boys."

Except by going to prison, but I didn't say so then. We would
get to that reality soon enough.

Ted's eyes, and the eyes of every man in the room, were on
me.

"I wouldn't recommend calling. I'd suggest a letter—an honest letter introducing yourself, your situation, your questions
about their school progress. You have a right to do so."

Ted slumped again. "My wife says I gave up all my rights when
I fell."

"Unless you signed a paper voluntarily giving up your parental
rights, they're still intact, and so are your responsibilities, which
include financial and emotional support."

Ted was shaking his head. He hadn't signed any such documents. At least twenty men were talking at once, building a raft of questions and floating it my way.

"Hey, guys, the course I've been hired to teach is Positive Parenting. If we get too far off task, you'll have more homework to do. I expect you to become familiar enough with the course material to spout sections of it to the MICC education counselor. I'm a contract employee; I walk a narrow line."

"We'll handle it, we'll handle everything you can give us."

"Man, it's about time somebody other than some old con said we had some rights."

"Anybody gives you any flack about this class, you let us know."

And so began parent education at McNeil Island Corrections Center. Twenty-five men completed the course with high grades. Many of them took several other courses with me through ensuing quarters. Ted, whose crimes were drug related, took every class I taught, some more than once.

Those twenty-five dads or stepdads had more than fifty children waiting for them to come home. I've forgotten the exact number, though it's noted somewhere in my old records. In one positive-parenting class a few years later, seventeen dads had seventy-six children with whom they corresponded. At the end of the century, over 1.5 million children nationwide had a parent in prison.

The MICC employee who misspelled parenting on my badge, and many like him, continued to discount the value of parent education and sneered at the books and curriculum I created, though there was never any evidence any of them read my work. So be it. They were wrong about children being better off with a parent in prison and uninformed about laws regarding parental rights.

The state must have clear and cogent reasons to file for termination of parental rights, and the parent must be given due process—legal representation and a court hearing. Though incarceration can be declared child abandonment, which is considered clear and cogent, that approach is rarely used. Most inmate parents go home to their families, their children. And therein lies my strongest argument for teaching parenting inside prison fences. It benefits the children.

As for Ted, he had legal and emotional rights to the benefits of a relationship with his sons, but the relationship was defined by his incarceration. He needed his wife's cooperation, or a court order, to so much as talk to them on the phone. Ted, like many incarcerated parents (fathers more often than mothers), had given in to a sense of powerlessness. His children suffered for it. With his new understanding of parental rights and responsibilities, he took the risk of contacting his sons' school.

Getting information about children's school records and performance can be a long and humbling process, but many inmate parents have undertaken it with satisfactory results. There were those in the general populace outside prison who didn't think inmates should have such rights and criticized me for teaching and writing guidelines for contacting school officials. Many teachers have thanked me. Most school administrators and teachers want to hear from incarcerated parents, if the parents contact them in an appropriate manner. They understand the emotional and scholastic impact an incarcerated parent has on a child, and they welcome an open and honest relationship with the parent. Still, schools must err on the side of caution when information is requested by anyone. Parents have to show proof of the relationship. Those incarcerated generally have to get a notarized affidavit about their crime and sentence from the prison administration.

The principal of the school Ted's sons attended was pleased to hear from him. Ted's wife wasn't so pleased, but it did precipitate more open communication between them. She sent Ted a letter ordering him to call her. He wrote down things he wanted to say to her. He told her it hurt him when she threw out the letters he wrote the boys. Then he said, "They'll find out. Someday they'll find out."

He told me later he knew it was a threat, and it bothered him.

On the scale of threats from prison, that one wouldn't cause a ping.

Before the quarter ended, Ted's wife started giving their boys the letters Ted wrote and agreed they could accompany their grandmother (Ted's mother) on visits. The boys wrote back. The first grader printed his name and drew a picture of himself. The third grader said he played T-ball and wanted his dad to come home to help him.

Ted and the other experimental class students gained information they had a right and responsibility to know. For the remainder of his incarceration, Ted wrote to his sons every week and sent them things he made: cards, small puzzles, simple crafts—all part of parenting course work. He left MICC once for work release and got sent back for a dirty urinalysis. According to him, he'd smoked one joint. He was housed at the MICC Annex, then an honor camp, which gave some credibility to his claim. He worked construction there during the day and came inside the main institution for whatever class I taught at night. Annex students were subjected to strip searches before coming inside. "If they want to look at me naked, let 'em," Ted said, "if it means I get to keep being a dad."

Teachers often don't know if they've made an impact on students. Ted said he'd keep me informed when he got out and called when he was back in court over child custody. He was divorced by then. Yes, he paid the court costs.

"Me and my ex are still duking it out over child custody and visitation," he said. (Remember, I taught parenting, not English.) "The boys like spending time with me, which pisses her off. The court wants verification of my parenting classes and grades, even though I gave my attorney everything. He says he needs a deposition."

Ted had given his attorney course syllabi, graded papers, official college transcripts, and a record of when he sent cards and letters to his sons. His attorney called me, said it looked good, and took a statement. Then the judge called, swore me in on the phone, and listened to my testimony.

Ted called a few days later. "I got shared custody and liberal visitation rights, and the boys keep their names." He laughed, sniffed a couple times, laughed again.

I sniffed too.

Ted's story is a nice one for a prison teacher to be able to tell. It was an easy case. Ted was legally married to the boys' mother when they were born. He'd financially supported the family until he went to jail, and during most of the time he was incarcerated. His crimes, all drug related, were low on the seriousness level of the state's criminal code. He had a supportive mother. All in all, Ted was a decent sort who got into drugs and learned a hard lesson.

Many stories aren't so nice. I hope to relate them with honesty and compassion, explain how each affected me, and demonstrate why the information might matter to others.

One last note on the experimental class: Someone at Pierce College questioned me about the official grade sheet. Where was the curve? How could every student do superior work?

What could I say? Parenting and family courses are not filled with absolutes—problems in which there's only one correct answer. I didn't deduct points for spelling, punctuation, or grammar. They were outstanding students, all twenty-five of them, including those who'd received pictures of my women students and used school notebook paper to write sexy letters. They earned their grades; I just recorded them.

4 Confronting Attitude

The success of Positive Parenting served as a bargaining chip, or wedge, in a scheme to implement a new orientation program at MICC. Associate superintendent (now superintendent) Alice Payne and then education director Tom Rabak (their real names), the two professional colleagues who enticed me to the island to coordinate the program, had a far-reaching project in mind: confront inmate attitude and rattle the foundation of the convict code.

Employees who would do the implementing groaned. They were burdened with an intensified case management program developed at DOC headquarters and an inmate population explosion. Someone said, "Enough, already." Alice, a petite, attractive blonde with Scandinavian determination, extensive corrections experience, and a look in her eye, pointed the forefinger of her right hand upward: she meant business.

When Tom introduced the program that he and Alice named Project Social Responsibility to the education team, he met similar resistance. Instructors and office personnel balked at the logistics: teachers' time, classroom space, increased paperwork. Tom, who'd grown accustomed to dissenters among his staff, listened to their arguments for a time, turned on his boyish smile, and said, "Just do it!"

The MICC superintendent, William Callahan (now retired), known for saying, "I will not warehouse men," had already signed off on the project and declared it mandatory for every man who arrived at McNeil Island. We went ahead, preparing to confront attitude.

Attitude, the old convict code, is the stuff prison movies use to let audiences know who really runs the joint. Old cons don't do "mandatory," they're doing prison: get out of their way, leave them alone, but make sure the chow's good, there's plenty of yard time, the phones are working, and mail gets delivered six days a week. "Orientation?" they said. "Man, this place sucks."

In some cases, dealing with old cons routed through Project Social Responsibility to their new confines in what was yet another old prison was easier than coercing DOC and education staff to participate in the program's delivery. Their comments regarding the system were more printable, but no less contemptuous. I faced a complex challenge.

But change was in the air. After problems in Washington state's prison system in the seventies and eighties, including three highly publicized heinous crimes committed by men on work-release status and one serious riot at the state penitentiary, the media-inspired taxpaying populace demanded that the Department of Corrections get tough on crime *now*. Washington, like most states, saw its prison population double during the nineties. Old cons accustomed to running prisons rubbed elbows with young, streetwise toughs from low-income inner-city areas where they sold drugs and generally did the rip-and-run. They joined forces with their homies inside. They were a different breed, with a different attitude.

Sprinkle in some white-collar offenders, some domestic abusers, some vehicular homicide convictions; stir them up and transport them to a medium-custody prison on an island in Puget Sound; and keep them in lockstep on chain day (Thursday) and orientation day (Friday) while they hone their attitude. Warn them to stay cool over the weekend, round them up again on Monday morning, deliver them to the education department, and give them one week to figure out how they're going to make prison work toward release and reintegration into a society that would just as soon throw away the key.

Therein rested the crux of my job: show all of them how to use prison time to prepare for successful reintegration into the real world. I was no longer just the parenting teacher, my favorite role. I was now Project Social Responsibility coordinator and chief confronter of attitude at McNeil Island Corrections Center. I met every chain on Friday, right behind the sergeant who said, "Listen up. It's mandatory. You mess up, you go to the Hole; when you get out, you go to PSR. Simple as that."

I met them again Monday morning and delivered eight hours of the twenty they spent in the week-long program. I earned a reputation early on as being tough but fair-minded, opinionated but interesting, old but not bad-looking. Looks are relative anywhere, especially in prison. Some called me the teacher with white hair; others the silver fox. No matter their games and cons, they didn't get much past me. I'd taught female felons for eleven years, a good training ground. Every corrections officer I met who had worked with both female and male felons said dealing with men was "a piece of cake" after coping with "the ladies."

I had help: twenty-nine DOC and education staff members, plus inmate teaching assistants (TAs) chosen for their prison moxie, test scores, and ability to translate for the growing Spanish-speaking population. Inmate TAs are critically important in prison classrooms. Many could do the teaching, and with education dollars tightening, they may take over more of those responsibilities. My first PSR teaching assistant, Rafael Gomez, was a decent and gentle man who spoke fluent Spanish and English and knew his way around the system. Inside the fence there are some things only inmates can accomplish. He served as a role model for new inmates without losing the respect of the old cons, and he often kept me from going into orbit.

Mr. Gomez was doing time for domestic violence, stabbing

his wife in a fit of jealousy. He was respected by other inmates for "being the man," and for "keeping his woman in line." In the months he served as the PSR TA, I never saw or heard a whisper of violence, and I wouldn't have known his crime had he not chosen to tell me. He's Hispanic; I would have guessed drug-related crimes, a stereotype, I admit. Outside the fence our paths would not have crossed. We lived in different worlds; I had little understanding of his, and I weighed cultural expectations in my evaluation of him. Domestic violence is not something I slough off as insignificant, but it didn't prevent me from liking, respecting, and relying on Rafael Gomez.

If I were to meet him now, in the free world, I'd give him a big hug.

In Washington state, all male inmates enter the system at Washington Corrections Center in Shelton, a dying lumber town. There they go through intensive testing and review for classification before being assigned to the prison where they'll start serving their time. Classification is the point-system process that determines an inmate's custody status. They start with points based on their crime, earn points by programming, lose points if they get infractions. If an inmate has too few points, custody is closed, and he is sent to an intensive management or close-custody prison with fewer privileges, closer surveillance, and little movement within the facility.

Many of the men who went through PSR started their time with medium-custody status for short to mid-range sentences of three to seven years, but there were a fair number on restricted-minimum status: their points were high but they still had too much time left to qualify for an honor camp placement. They'd been convicted of more serious crimes, had done time at a close-custody institution, and were getting closer to release. Some of them had been around and seen it all, and after verbal expressions of displeasure, employed nonverbal tactics meant to intimidate mere mortals such as teachers. When they couldn't stare me down, they turned and stared out the windows. I left what some presenters considered the safety of the lectern and made my way to their chair desks, to make eye contact and start some nonthreatening dialogue.

"What do you see out there? Deer browsing just outside the fence? Lucky deer, they come and go as they please."

Invariably someone snickered. A snicker beats a sneer every time. I prowled the room, looking at badges and making comments that included DOC numbers, posture, and attempts to push chair desks through the back wall or drag them out the door into the hallway. All my antics and delays were designed to give the teeming testosterone time to settle.

Sometimes, to rouse curiosity, gain empathy, or get their eyes off the clocks, I told them one of my early MICC experiences. "I was in the main corridor waiting to go through key control when someone tapped me on the shoulder and said, 'Let me see your badge.' I turned, expecting a security officer, and found a man in civilian clothes, reeking of cigarettes and glowering. 'I thought so,' he said. 'Yellow badge, bleeding heart, nose-wiping do-gooder. You ought to go back to teaching kindergarten.' Actually, he said 'kiddie garden.' Then he postured for a group of onlookers. He discounted my worth without knowing me. Just for the record, I don't wipe noses, but Mr. Gomez does keep toilet paper in the classroom in case any of us need it." They generally laughed, and someone almost always said, "Dude in the story's a dumb fuck." I'd agree, ignoring the language or sometimes frowning, and we'd carry on.

Most of the men newer to the system were more cooperative than the old cons. New inmates had just suffered the inertia of jail, and then the restrictions of Shelton's receiving unit, where they went through psychological tests and health probes done with army-like sensitivity. They were ready to settle somewhere and make the best of a bad situation. Getting settled meant more privileges, including visitation and phone calls, recreation, education, and possibly a job that would let them buy "store": tobacco and papers; candy, chips, and soda; better quality personal hygiene items than those provided by the state.

I'd been dancing to the concertina's tune long enough to have invented a few steps, and I learned new ones as the PSR program evolved. Rigidity does not succeed in education, parenting, or any viable relationship. We were trying to lay a foundation with the men to garner their cooperation, a process DOC's case management required. Abandonment, rigidity's opposite, was another problem we needed to counter in PSR to make the program succeed. Prison is a rigid environment where many feel (and frequently have been) abandoned by society at large, and all too often by family and friends who find maintaining a relationship too emotionally taxing.

Imagine someone you love is in prison. Imagine a relatively short sentence of sixty months, with one-third off for good behavior. The person will do forty months in a corrections facility. How many of the approximately twelve hundred days will you subject yourself to the stress of prison visiting? How many collect phone calls will you accept? How often will you write a letter?

I've seen the pain, not just the anger, of those locked away. I've shielded crying men from others' eyes. Still, I never forgot that my students came to the classroom and program via criminal acts. It was my job to help them change, not to coddle them.

After the first two hours with a new group, the entire PSR team met to discuss behavior patterns I'd observed, possible problems that might occur back in the cell house or in other facets of the program, what parts of our vast curriculum might be most helpful, what might meet the most resistance. We learned early on that even the toughest old cons were impressed by the number and the status of presenters who came to them: associate superintendents, correctional program managers, a security captain, lieutenants, sergeants, correctional officers, a prison job coordinator, a grievance coordinator, a disciplinary hearings officer, an education director, academic and vocational teachers, education support staff, living-unit supervisors and counselors, a psychiatric social worker, a chemical dependency counselor, hospital staff, and chapel staff.

Most of us on the team gave it our all. We played up the "star value" of those presenters who generally weren't seen on the education floor. We reminded those men they would return to their families and communities, where they'd need to integrate with all who'd never seen the inside of a prison, and who had little empathy for offenders.

Wind blew onto the island from the sound, hummed through the concertina wire, and set the rhythm for our work. Week after week we performed for a new crowd—a new chain that gathered at the cell house sergeant's desk when the intercom crackled to life and a voice announced, "Period movement, period movement."

We danced as fast as we could.

5 Roles, Rules, and Realities

Men had ten minutes to get from their living units to their program areas when period movement was announced. They swarmed out of the old cell house (the same place I'd visited all those years ago) into the prison's main passageway. Those destined for education climbed a flight of stairs from the corridor; those among them mandated to attend Project Social Responsibility came looking for coffee we'd promised as a little bonus, a little balance to the mandate. Some drank coffee only as an excuse for sugar. We never had enough. Sugar packets were swooped up; artificial sweetener packets accumulated. I couldn't find a spare granule of the real thing anywhere. Education staff hid their supply after my first raid. Sugar is a drug, a substitute for the illegal ones the men would prefer. Six, ten, twelve, sixteen packets of sugar in a Styrofoam cup, with enough coffee to dissolve it. Those in first grabbed fast. Those who were late complained.

"Sorry, it's gone," I'd say, and raise my left eyebrow when they suggested I should contact the kitchen for more. Sometimes, when I look in the mirror, I think that eyebrow is permanently higher than the other.

Nor would I stand by the coffee urn and monitor use. They

caught on. They'd either get there earlier or risk palming and pocketing sugar packets elsewhere.

Coffee was a nice idea, but it would become an increasing problem. Spilled coffee, empty sugar packets, and pieces of Styrofoam littered the floor. Inmate porters (the janitorial crew) resented cleaning up after those who were careless and complained to their bosses, education floor officers, who sided with them. Part of the rub was coffee, and on Mondays and Fridays cookies to boot. Those porters didn't get any of the goodies, and they overheard enough staff grumbling on the education floor and throughout the institution to know the PSR program wasn't unanimously supported even by all who worked to make it happen.

One porter said, "Man, I ain't cleanin' up after no slob for twenty-six cents an hour," starting wage for most institution jobs in the nineties.

Eliminating coffee would be one of the first changes in the program.

The porters had another complaint: I didn't make the men keep their chair desks in straight rows. Getting comfortable, rearranging furniture, and stretching out helped the program work. I laughed the first time I heard the complaint and groaned and shook my head to indicate my pique the second. The third time, I swallowed a couple pejoratives about porters and one or two DOC staff and said, "Oh, for God's sake, I'll arrange the damn things myself."

Mr. Gomez stepped in. He calmed my nerves, straightened the room, cleaned the blackboard, translated for Spanish-speaking men, set up files, kept up with the mounds of paperwork, brought me ice water he got from a kitchen connection, decorated the classroom with odd bits of things he or I procured, watered plants, and found containers for the flowers I brought from home. He had a certain dignity, an appreciation for niceties that created a pleasant atmosphere in the classroom. I don't know where he found vases inside an old prison, but once he brought them to our room, we kept them there, and I tried to keep them filled. It made a difference. Mr. Gomez made a difference. I could rely on a subtle smile, nod, or look in his eyes when the going got rough.

Once the men got their coffee, appraised my antics of the day, and settled down, Mr. Gomez distributed folders with a program schedule, notebook paper, and a pencil inside, and we got to work. We started Monday morning with a session on roles, rules, and individual responsibility. There each sat in state-issued khaki pants and shirt, white T-shirt showing, khaki jacket draped over the back of the chair, khaki watch cap stuffed into a pocket, khaki belt cinched if the pants were too large.

Someone always said, "Roles? We're inmates, that's our role." Generally they said "fucking inmates," and "fucking role," to which I'd raise my eyebrow before saying, "And students," thus provoking the first argument of the day. Not all saw themselves as students, even though they'd signed a Pierce College registration form and wanted the promised certificate of completion and course credits for the program.

We built a list from there. Son, father, brother, uncle, husband or partner, lover, employee—the list went on. When I said "lover," they narrowed their eyes. They wanted to see what I said as much as hear it. They listened when I talked about showing love from a distance. Some scoffed, but they listened. I suspect they hadn't met many women inside the system who talked about emotional intimacy versus phone sex, a staple of prison life. Some blushed. Sometimes I blushed. I'm Scandinavian; it's easy to tell when my face reddens.

They were warmed up to the notion of classroom discussion by the time Alice Payne or another associate superintendent came in to talk about the institution's expectations of them. Even the toughest cons admitted they were surprised someone would come down out of the ivory tower, interact with them with respect, listen to them, answer their questions, and try to learn their names. A small thing, you may think, but in education it's often the small thing, the seemingly insignificant moment, that matters the most. In prison the impact is increased twofold, tenfold, maybe even a hundredfold. Inmates have been condemned for their criminal acts. Most of them need reminders, often just simple indications, of their own humanity.

They sat up straighter, but went silent, when the shift lieutenant entered. Those in khaki do not trust those in blue, and Lieutenant Burton had a tough-guy persona earned by performance of his duties—his role. He'd grown up in the projects of a Pittsburgh suburb, fought in Korea and Vietnam, and worked at McNeil Island when it was still a federal prison. He'd strut across the front of the old classroom, point his finger, spout clichés, and say, "Equal worth as humans does not mean equal power in every situation," a line he'd heard me say and adopted as his own. The men listened and nodded. It was an important concept, and it worked better coming from him, another male and one with power. They needed to see me as a Pierce College instructor, not as the law.

The lieutenant and I started out on a bad note over his finger-pointing habit and his general resentment of the extra work the program caused his officers. Unlike Alice Payne, who pointed at the ceiling, Burton pointed at the person. He whipped up his arm like he was drawing a gun, pointed his finger, and crooked it once; and the pointee came as if lassoed and pulled in. I'd been advised to get the lieutenant on board our PSR team, to get him to drop in at least long enough to show the men we had his support. Getting him to do that much wasn't easy, and next thing I knew, Alice Payne asked me to get Lieutenant Burton more involved.

Cajoling staff to serve as backup for our main program presenters became part of my job. I went to the lieutenant, epitome of traditional male privilege, with a proposal that he join me in a presentation on male roles in the nineties. I suspected playing off his rigidity might work with those equally stuck male inmates. Of course, the lieutenant resisted. I had no intention of getting into a power struggle, so I told him we would like his support and left the decision to him. We had another lieutenant, one who handled inmate disciplinary hearings, involved in the project. This was adequate lieutenant representation, it seemed to me. I had other responsibilities: regular college classes to teach, a PSR training manual to write, other programs in the planning stage. My cajoling time was limited.

I was in the corridor, the prison's main artery, dashing from a meeting with the associate superintendent to Education, when the lieutenant and I had our set-to. I had a parenting class to teach in five minutes and wanted to grab a few bites of lunch, use the restroom, and find the proper stack of materials to haul to which-ever classroom was available. The shift lieutenant's office was across the corridor from the stairs to Education. The corridor offi-cer saw me coming and walked to the stairwell door, key in hand to let me through. She'd be announcing period movement in a matter of minutes. Lieutenant Burton strolled into the corridor, pointed at me, crooked his finger, and sauntered back toward his office.

"The lieutenant wants you," the CO said.

"I don't respond to beckoning fingers. I have a name." I knew he could hear me. If I'd addressed myself directly to him, he'd have heard a good deal more.

She frowned, but unlocked the door. "It's not a good idea to ignore the lieutenant."

"Maybe not for you, but I work for Pierce College, not the lieutenant."

I was halfway up the stairs—on the first landing—when I heard him call my name. I turned and glared and forgot all my resolve not to get into a power struggle. "Do not ever point your finger at me. I consider it demeaning."

He nodded and laughed a contagious laugh. "Jan, will you please come to my office for a minute?"

I was Jan, he was Lieutenant Burton. He held the power and was now condescending to me. I declined, with what seemed a reasonable excuse.

"I have a two-hour class to teach, and I haven't had any lunch."

"It will only take a minute."

I was on the spot. The project needed him; one female officer was watching (and grinning, but he couldn't see her); and several male officers had gathered in the corridor. I started back down the steps, vowing I would not continue if he turned his back and left me to follow. He didn't. He waited, and while he waited he pointed his finger at one of the male officers.

"You, go on up to Education and meet her class so she can eat her lunch."

That's how it's done. The officer reared back, stunned. "Me? Teach her class?"

"Did I say teach her class? Or did I say meet her class? Take attendance. You can handle that, right?"

"Right, LT, right."

Students in our program answered much the same way when the lieutenant spoke to them. He'd give them his lieutenant look. "I'll bet most of you have said, 'Sometimes a man's gotta do what a man's gotta do.' Am I right?" He'd get nods. "Well, it's the same with the system. My officers gotta do what they gotta do. You follow the rules, you'll be okay. They jack you up for something you don't have coming, you let me know. They nail you when you're out of line, don't come whining to me. Take it like a man. Right?"

"Right, LT, right."

Who but a black lieutenant with a tough-guy reputation could have accomplished so much with such a simple speech? His presence on Monday morning told those men MICC security sanctioned the program, but some of the things he said made me cringe. Cringe and grin, too. Something about those men got to him. He agreed to help with the afternoon program. I'm not certain what made him give in and decide to join us, but I have long suspected he liked how I dealt with him, and the inmates.

On his Monday morning forays into the classroom he'd say, "This program's mandatory, but that doesn't make it *all* bad. I've been listening to her" [he'd point his finger at me] and I've learned a lot. You listen up; you might get something out of this."

Then he'd stroll to the classroom door, stop, point at the men. "I'll be back this afternoon."

Perhaps we were two of a kind: we liked the classroom theater.

The Male Roles in the '90s session was a quick look at expectations placed on men through the century, what had changed, and where it left men in relation to women and society. In Lieutenant Burton we got the traditional male we needed: a rigid, obstinate, inveterate officer. He agreed to participate in the project only if someone developed curriculum and a lesson plan for him to use. I wrote it, explained what we wanted and needed from him, coaxed and coached. He never used it. I doubt he ever looked at it; he just followed my lead as I introduced the topic. At times I felt like the straight person in a stand-up comedy act. I provided the material; the lieutenant provided the levity. When we got into male sex-role conditioning, a major area of my master's thesis research some years back, the lieutenant bloomed. Jungian therapist and author Jean Shinoda Bolen would call him an Ares Man, an archetypal warrior, dancer, and lover. By dancer she meant a physical rather than mental man. The lieutenant couldn't be bothered with preparing the materials we presented, or even writing on the board. While I lectured and wrote, he moved about the room interrupting me, expanding on a notion I put forth, a sociological fact, a bit of history. Ares men are reactive, and they lust for battle. Pity the inmate who wanted to argue with the lieutenant, unless the man hooked his father instinct, another Ares trait personified in the lieutenant by how he handled the officers who answered to him. He issued orders with a pointing finger and clipped words, and he carried their personal crises around as a pre-ulcer and high blood pressure.

A shift lieutenant runs the security side of a prison while he's on duty. Every sergeant and corrections officer on every post is his responsibility; every inmate his charge; every employee and visitor on prison property his concern. The lieutenant took his job seriously. Now and then he'd complain, in the privacy of my office, that things were easier when he didn't meet every inmate face-to-face; when they were just names and numbers. It got harder to order a man removed from open population to administrative segregation—the Hole—when it was a man he'd met in Project Social Responsibility.

Together the lieutenant and I painted a picture of how sex roles changed with history beginning with the early 1900s. While I wrote key terms on the board—*Depression, World War II, Korea, civil rights movement, Vietnam, Watergate*—the lieutenant and inmates talked about how men saw themselves during those times. But when we moved from those tangible moments in history to sociological change, the lieutenant said, "That's her department." I'd write *advent of television, sexual revolution, increasing divorce, drug abuse, spousal abuse, child abuse, increasing crime,* or *AIDS,* and ask how they affected male sex roles.

"You answer her," the lieutenant said, and if no one did he'd point his finger at a man and say, "You, that's an order, you answer now."

For all his insistence that those topics were my department, he warmed to the task of teaching them, and interrupted me often. He didn't agree with all of my views, and sometimes he pointed his finger and called me opinionated. I'd narrow my eyes and point back. He'd laugh.

When the intercom snapped to life and a voice announced, "Period movement, period movement," the ten-minute break provided each hour on the half-hour during the prison program day, there were always men who groaned. They didn't want it to end. When I look back on those sessions, I suspect some of those men thought they'd found a set of parents—a firm, traditional father and an informed, liberated mother. Others thought they'd stumbled into a road show, a diversion from the boredom of prison. I remember it as exhausting, but oddly successful. At the very least we gave them material for thought.

The lieutenant left the floor laughing. If I was lucky, I managed to use the restroom and grab a drink of water before the next hour, a heavier one with an ulterior motive. Critical thinking was a major component of the project, and we hoped to stimulate such thinking before an instructor formally introduced the concept the next morning. We used the George Orwell essay "Shooting an Elephant" to accomplish our goal. It should have been a natural segue after what they'd experienced with Lieutenant Burton, but what seems logical to a group of prison administrators and educators planning a program isn't always what works with inmates.

The essay was a favorite of Tom Rabak, the education director who had worked so hard to make Project Social Responsibility a reality. Early on he and I worked together to present the material and lead a discussion. He soon turned the task over to me, and shortly afterward he left MICC for an opportunity to work with younger students who still had a chance to avoid prison.

The essay may have been a bit of an intellectual stretch for inmate students: many overidentified with the elephant and considered the author a pitiful dude.

6 Orwell's Elephant

George Orwell's essay "Shooting an Elephant" appears in many literary anthologies and is widely used in high school and college English literature classes to teach narration and description. For our use in Project Social Responsibility, we compared Orwell's discomfort and ensuing behavior in a place strange to him with inmates' unease when plunged into the prison environment. We drew a parallel and asked the men to ponder other choices Orwell might have made. Though some of our team members argued the essay was beyond the reach of most of our students (statistics suggest 70 percent of prison inmates nationwide are illiterate), Tom Rabak argued that most would comprehend if the work was read aloud and discussed.

He and I plowed ahead as a tag team, defining unfamiliar words and terms; reading aloud, providing copies for those who wanted to follow along; urging them to think about the reason for Orwell's decision. When Tom's director duties called him to meetings, many off-island, I handled the presentation alone. In truth the men accepted me more readily than Tom: I'd been with them for several hours and become a known factor.

"Shooting an Elephant" relates an experience Orwell had while in service with the imperial police in Burma in the early

1920s. Those familiar with Orwell's *Animal Farm* and *Nineteen Eighty-four* know his incensed attitude toward repressive government, imperialism, and despots. He was nineteen or twenty at the time he left English university to serve the British Commonwealth as a police officer in Burma rather than complete his education, and he found himself loathed and ridiculed by the Burmese. He opens the essay by stating he was hated by large numbers of people, the only time in his life he was important enough for that to happen.

For our purposes we started with the essay's third paragraph, where Orwell moves from describing his position to narrating the event, which he calls a tiny incident in itself. An elephant has gone "must," broken its chain, and escaped its handler, and it is ravaging the marketplace. It has already destroyed a bamboo hut, killed a cow, and overturned a rubbish van and "inflicted violences upon it." As a police officer, he is called on to do something about the elephant and sets out on a pony to see what is happening.

The men generally liked that the elephant was being influenced by an attack of "must," which we defined for them as rut, a word they knew. They could identify with a male being a little out of control under such circumstances. There would be some chest beating, a high five here and there, a little bragging. Then they asked exactly what violences were inflicted on the rubbish van. The bamboo hut and killed cow were of less interest.

In the next paragraph, Orwell describes the area where the elephant has been seen, and moves to the discovery of a man trampled to death, his arms crucified and his back skinned. Some of the men found that quite to their liking; others saw it as racist, since Orwell calls the dead man a black Dravidian (Indian) coolie. We learned, in time, to prepare them properly for the coolie's ethnicity, and to teach a little geography and history before I read the story.

Orwell paints a picture of the place: the squalor, the crowd of two thousand or so that is growing. The power of the crowd seeking excitement convinces Orwell he will have to shoot the elephant. He doesn't want to for several reasons, none of which have to do with killing an animal. The elephant has a greater worth alive than dead. Killing it is akin to destroying a valuable piece of machinery, but not killing it will leave him looking a fool. That is what he cannot permit. He shoots the elephant. It is a disastrous shot, as are the subsequent ones; the elephant takes half an hour to die and then is stripped to the bones for its meat.

Orwell shot the forward part of the elephant's massive head, thinking the brain would be there. He later learned he should have aimed for the ear hole. In preparing to use the essay, I made a trip to Tacoma's Point Defiance Zoo to see the elephants and study their anatomy and demeanor. I needed to see their heads in profile and to gauge the distance between their eyes and ears, to understand Orwell's dilemma. That kind of investigation, I believe, is a necessity of teaching.

Orwell violated his personal values to protect his worth in the eyes of a crowd he despised. He did what the crowd expected someone in his role as British officer to do, and in the act lost rather than protected his sense of self-worth. Orwell wrote that in such acts, in his case becoming the oppressor against his better judgment, a man destroys his own freedom. I considered the story's most telling line to be "He wears a mask, and his face grows to fit it." In fact that line, and the essay's closing, in which he admits his motive—shooting the elephant "solely to avoid looking a fool"—did trigger thinking and discussion with many of the men. Some drifted off into quiet thought, which I honored by not pushing them to talk.

When it worked best, inmates drew the parallel we intended: Correctional officers were sometimes pushed to behave in certain ways because of the badges they wore, the expectations heaped on them. Many inmates had been "acting out" for attention, position, a sense of power, for much of their lives. They groused about "the man" jerking them around and had no inkling that negative attention satisfied their need and drove them to continue acting out. I'd watch their eyes as awareness settled, notice little frowns furrow foreheads, or heads lower so no one could see too far into their own recognition: they had hurt others, and in the act hurt themselves.

The stage was set for Tuesday's critical thinking session, so pertinent to personal crime reexamination. We were working toward our goal and helping our students prepare for their future choices. In the process we introduced the value of literature in learning and possibly inspired some men to read something other than men's magazines at the prison library.

But some of the time getting to the lesson's objective was a lot like rowing upstream with broken oars.

In the early weeks of PSR, one man sobbed so hard my teaching assistant had to procure an additional roll of toilet paper from the men's restroom—an infractionable offense if he was caught. We generally acquired our supply when the janitorial closet was open and kept an extra roll of the rough tissue locked in a file cabinet for the next time we needed it.

The sobbing man caught me off guard as he gulped and asked, "Why did the elephant have to die?" Tears streamed from his eyes and mucus from his nose.

"Don't pay him no mind," another man said. "He's crazy."

He may have been. Many inmates do have mental problems, and in another time would have been housed in a mental facility rather than prison. It was also common for a man to make such an announcement. Craziness went with the territory, and no one seemed offended when someone pointed it out. I felt duty-bound to offer the distraught man comfort, a difficult task to accomplish with just words. Touch, even a brief encounter of my fingers and his skin, could convey the wrong message. I used my ever-present but just-under-the-surface mothering skills and watched those teary eyes beg for more. He would have climbed onto my lap if I'd offered it.

Now and then a man in the group thought the story was a warning: they'd be shot, literally or figuratively, if they got out of line. I heard lengthy, rather logical diatribes on the unfairness of infractions and sanctions for things they likened to an elephant's tipping over a rubbish van—things such as wasting food or supplies, stealing a piece of toast from Mainline (prison dining hall), smoking where prohibited.

One week a man compared the elephant's shooting to a crime scene and kept right on extolling the glory of blood and gore when I said, "Stop!" I wound my way through the classroom tangle to stand in front of him. He kept on, lost in another place, an ugly place. I smothered his words with my own. "Stop. No more. The end. You will not continue with your story. Do you hear me? Stop now." It was one of the most graphic tales I heard during my tenure, and I listened to or overheard many, most of them exaggerations and fantasies. Inmates, like disturbed veterans of war, tend to borrow others' experiences and embroider on them for status within the system.

"Huh?" the man said when he felt me standing there. He struggled to get his eyes in focus.

Now and then men remembered hunting trips for deer, elk, bear, and squirrels if they were from Missouri, crocodiles if they were from Louisiana. They were fifth graders at camp, out-telling the last tall tale.

It's fortunate that I like men in general, was reared by a father who hunted, and had reared sons of my own.

No matter how well our discussion went, it always ended with one or two men upset over the elephant's death. They were still talking about it the next day, and many came by my classroom weeks and months later to mention the dead elephant, stripped to the bones for its meat. Soon the new chain of men, who heard about the story from cell mates during their "free" weekend before PSR, asked about the elephant first thing Monday morning.

By the time the intercom announced period movement to end PSR's first full day and Mr. Gomez straightened the classroom, I felt as though I'd wrestled an elephant. I'd spent four hours interacting with the new chain and one hour in a meeting about them. To the best of my knowledge, I was a pioneer. There were Department of Corrections personnel who had been in the same room with a group of inmates monitoring tests and distributing information for long stretches, but interaction was minimal. I was a guide on uncharted terrain, still scoffed at by naysayers, occasionally heralded by Project Social Responsibility team members. My empathy for Orwell's Burma experience deepened with each presentation of his essay.

In a sense, I became part of each chain. I was stuck with them and they with me. Once the week ended, we could all get on with what we were in prison to do, which for me was teaching various and sundry parenting and family classes and dealing with the next chain, and the next, reading them Orwell's account of shooting that poor randy elephant.

1 Visiting the Cell House

The old cell house at McNeil Island, now replaced by modern, state-of-the-art living units, was legendary when I first transferred to MICC. Lieutenant Burton, that stalwart man who'd grown up tough and fought in two wars, professed it housed ghosts of men who died ugly deaths there. We were alone in his office, a safe place for such stories. The change in his eyes told me he felt reverence for the place much as he might for a chapel. An officer came through the door, and the lieutenant's story switched to slipping in the trail of a dying federal inmate's blood, unable to catch up with the man to escort him to the prison hospital.

There were other times when Lieutenant Burton permitted a glimpse of his emotional side for a moment, then closed the curtain and went into good ol' boy mode. In time, I discovered other officers operated in similar ways. It went with the territory. In quiet moments, when they weren't being observed or overheard, several officers who'd been around in federal days spoke of a cell no longer used because it housed the devil, or remnants of devil worship—the story varied with the teller. Those who knew its history best feared something untoward would happen in the process of demolishing it. (To my knowledge, nothing did, though there were reports of things going bump in the night.)

I visited it soon after transferring to the island and went there occasionally to meet with an inmate counselor during the early days of Project Social Responsibility. Those counselors' offices were well-lighted, comfortable places when compared to the cells, but bleak and undesirable if measured by any other standard for office space. They made the ugly classrooms on the Education floor, and my long, narrow office, which was either too hot or too cold, seem luxurious.

All new employees received an island tour, which included walking the tiers of cell blocks to get a taste of how our clients lived. Electronic controls already opened and closed most prison gates by then, but the cell house still had a gearwheel and racking system, and it required a trained officer to maneuver a large lever to drop gears in place.

Tom Rabak acted as my escort, an unusual occurrence since neither of us was directly employed by the DOC. The gate officer didn't hesitate to rack the doors. He expected us, explained how the gate worked, and gave a little tour-guide speech about the age and architecture of the old monstrosity and the state's plans to tear it down. He said that more than nine hundred cots and mattresses, even those in perfectly good condition, would be destroyed along with the building. (I heard that fact bandied about when the wrecker's ball went to work. Destroying so many mattresses, and replacing them with similar mattresses simply because old ones weren't to be used in the new living units, irked many long-time prison employees.)

Tom and I walked tiers, my pumps ringing on steps as we climbed or descended, warning inmates a woman was in the blocks. (I wore running shoes to and from the island: it made navigating boat ramps and docks, and the long hill and many stairs, easier; but I hadn't thought to change into them before going into the blocks.)

Some men lined up at the bars of their cells to watch us, to call out greetings or jeers. Others slept or read. Men who'd been permitted out for showers moved around us. One man turned to allow me full view of his hirsute chest, which he offered with a wink. For a moment I thought he would offer more, but modesty or a nearby officer prevailed. I disliked being there, a voyeur in a private world of macho males. Some female officers thrived on cell-house duty: they liked the sense of power and fought their unions and DOC for the right to perform professional duties equally with men. In my case it interfered with the teacher/student relationship.

Somewhere on our tour we bumped into a prison program administrator I'll call Hal. By his position, he should have been one of the main players in our PSR pageant, but he avoided taking an active part. He walked along with us, lamenting the reality of the old building's pending demise. He liked the dark dankness, the overcrowded conditions, the caged-animal atmosphere.

Hal went from love of the old cell house to dislike of Project Social Responsibility. The new case management requirements were bad enough, already overwhelming his counseling staff, and now this worthless orientation program had been foisted on them by Alice Payne and a bunch of teachers who weren't capable of doing real work. (How many times did I hear an MICC employee recant the old "Those who can, do . . ."?)

Hal personified the bureaucrat who is discomfited by change and sees those involved in bringing it about as personal foes. He ignored Tom's friendly grin and my charming smile, uttered another string of strong negative adjectives about PSR, and said to me, "You're just another newbie; you don't know from nothing; you drive up here with a green face and try to make changes that ain't gonna work."

We kept walking, but I've long been able to talk and walk at the same time, and I let my mouth get away from me. "Actually, I didn't drive; I came by boat like everyone else." I knew better. In addition to extensive training in my field, child and family studies, I have certificates in related areas, including negotiation and mediation. But reticence is not one of my virtues, and being attacked by MICC hard-liners wore on me.

Hal's eyes narrowed. Tom put a hand on my arm. "Jan's been

teaching in the system for over eleven years. She's not a newbie; she's pioneered other programs . . ."

Hal's face moved so close he consumed our share of the stale cell-house air. "Yeah, so I keep hearing, women's prison. Big fucking deal. A handful of fucked-up women in a dinky prison that looks like a college campus. She's a green-face, an Alice Payne flunky, and she don't know from nothin' when it comes to men."

I opened my mouth to fire another round—truths about working with female felons, research on male sex-role conditioning— but noticed the echo of Hal's words still bounced off the cell-house walls. We'd made it back to the gate by then. The officer who manned the gears watched. Standing a post for hours on end gets boring. A little verbal battle is a nice distraction. I'm often outspoken, but not dumb. It was time to close my mouth and depart.

"Nice bumping into you, Hal," I said, and thanked the officer for racking the doors so we could escape.

Word of our meeting spread through the prison. Only four of us were right there: Tom, Hal, the officer who racked the cell-house gears, and I. Four of us, a few hundred inmates, and some unit officers and counselors tucked into cubbyholes or walking a tier. The prison wireless is a reality inside the fence. Want to know what will be on tomorrow's Daily Transfer Sheet? Ask an inmate today.

Hal did not like the news of our brief encounter making insider-gossip headlines. He got razzed over the "newbie with a green face" comment. I had an enemy.

In the following months, changes ran rampant at MICC, all in the name of capital improvement to rid the island of the old cell house and bring living conditions up to standards approved by watchdog agencies. New living units were under construction just beyond the old cell-house perimeter. The chapel, now in the construction zone, closed; services were moved to another building. Education classrooms closed for a time too, for asbestos removal, so we met in odd spots.

Change unsettles inmates. Even those who looked forward to

modern living units suffered the unrest in the cell house, where the old convict code still ruled in ways I'd never understand. It made integration of the weekly chain even more difficult. Our PSR meetings served as alerts for potential problems. Our team members grew increasingly weary and asked for more backup staff to take off the pressure. The Department of Corrections transferred Alice Payne, the dynamic associate superintendent and originator of the project, to headquarters. Tom Rabak, our education director, left soon after. I'd lost my strongest support.

That's when Hal struck. He filed a sexual harassment grievance against me. It arrived in my hands via the new education director, a man who had made it clear he would not take an active part in PSR, and I swear he smirked when he delivered the formal document.

I read it and laughed. "Sexual harassment? For what?"

"You speak down to him in meetings. Specifically, you stood, looked right at him, and said something like it's time for him to take an active role, to take over one of the presentations."

"Speaking to him while standing is sexual harassment?"

The new education director grinned. "Men do not like aggressive women."

"I'm not interested in being 'liked' by Hal."

"Maybe you played your cards wrong."

Of course I had played my cards wrong. It's not even complex, when looked at in sequence. Alice Payne had been Hal's immediate supervisor and had ordered him to participate in Project Social Responsibility. He did the minimum: he attended our weekly meetings. Tom Rabak had worked with Alice to bring the project to life. Both were my friends. What Hal and the new education director saw as aggressive I'd define as assertive, but those are just words.

The words Hal quoted me as using, when he filed his grievance, were, "Hal, you're the only person still uncommitted."

The DOC sent a female investigator to interview us, separately, before making a ruling. She said, "Maybe the commitment word made it sexual." We analyzed the word's meaning: emotional binding together, as in relationships; pledge to do something; confining to prison. Hmm.

Sometime later an official document stamped "Grievance denied" arrived. It was addressed to me and marked "Personal." I found it in my staff mailbox, already opened.

Hal never did take an active role in PSR. He and the old cell house stayed bound together in my mind. Archaic, antiquated, needing to be replaced. Now and then Hal and I passed in the corridor, or on our way to the boat at the end of the workday, and he greeted me as though nothing unusual had transpired between us. When a position opened in one of the new minimum-custody work camp facilities in eastern Washington, Hal asked for a transfer.

I was one of a few staff not invited to his farewell party, which delighted me. It was so pointed a slight. Lieutenant Burton took one look at the grin I couldn't hide, laughed, and told me to leave it alone. I think that meant he was on my side.

8 The Chain and Its Links

In some odd way, my interactions and experiences with Hal made me more empathetic toward new arrivals at McNeil Island and participants in Project Social Responsibility. I've spoken of them as the chain, a collective identity that followed them from Thursday arrival through the entire following week in PSR. In my early years at MICC, the men on the chain, dressed in orange coveralls, came on the regular ferry, on the 8:40 A.M. run. I rode the 7:25 shift boat and usually avoided seeing men in shackles.

Usually—except for the morning the Pierce College video production crew shot footage of a chain arrival for our Project Social Responsibility video presentation.

The chain waits until other passengers have disembarked and headed for their workstations or homes. When it's their turn, the chain moves like a giant orange centipede, down the ramp from the ferry's gaping port-side door onto the float; across the float and up the long gangplank onto the dock; along the dock and up the sidewalk, single file, in perfect step to keep from tripping. Hands cuffed at their waist fronts and connected by chain to the waist back ahead; ankles cuffed, connected, clinking against planks and then cement. Officers with them, fore and aft; officers watching from the towers; officers waiting at R&D, Receiving and Delivery.

The photographer/producer caught the contrast: the beauty of Puget Sound with sunlight reflecting on its surface, the long pier jutting out from the rocky McNeil Island shore, the float and creosote-covered pilings, the ferry cutting a wide swath and making a perfect portside landing. Snow-clad and pristine Mount Rainier in the distance, looming above a black-green forest. Orange coverall–clad men in body chains.

By the time I met the chain in the PSR classroom, the actual chains had been removed, and the men were able to move about as individuals—as long as they met prison rules and expectations. It still bothered me to see another human in chains, a regular event at McNeil Island, where inmates being escorted to off-island medical care travel in chains, often with two officers guarding them. The sight dredged up the loss of self I'd felt so many years before, when I'd been a guest on the island for a short time, and trussed up to entertain my community college students. The reality of chains, of the chain, interfered with my determination to meet inmates in the prison classroom as students equal to those in any other classroom.

Responsibilities in my role as PSR coordinator had a long reach. I needed to face the chain's reality.

Gates and doors open for them and clang shut behind, until they're inside the basement R&D room where processing begins. Receiving and Delivery. Processing. A commodity. Words carry clout.

The men are cold or hot, depending on the weather and the idiosyncrasies of an old building's heating system. Their wrists and ankles are sore; their arms, legs, and backs strained; their sweat and breath rancid. They need haircuts. They need the restroom.

An officer produces a key, starts unlocking chains. What does he feel as he frees those individuals from their bondage to all the others? Another officer collects the chains, keeps them from tangling. They clank, producing an odd rhythm. I hear it as discordant plunking on a cheap guitar.

There are brown folding chairs arranged for the men. An officer orders them to sit.

"Man, I need to piss."

A thumb is jerked, indicating a restroom. "Make it quick, we're running late here."

There are twenty-one men in orange coveralls, most rubbing first one wrist and then the other. There are a handful of officers—one sergeant, the rest line staff. There's me, in a navy-blue tailored suit, skirt below my knees, and navy pumps; my conservative outfit for such an austere occasion. I've been advised (read that ordered) to be here, to see how it works. I'm out of place, worse than a voyeur. I've seen enough, but I don't leave. I'm introduced; I nod and smile. I want to close my eyes. My chest is tight, partly with empathy, partly with memory of a time I'd come close to acting a fool. I think about Orwell. In a few days I'll be reading the essay to this group. Will I tell them how I felt at this moment?

Somewhere there are mothers wondering about their sons, and how they're being treated on this day, their transport day from the Washington Corrections Center at Shelton to the McNeil Island Corrections Center.

Somewhere there are victims wondering about their victimizers, and how they're being treated on this day.

I think about them and swallow. It sounds loud.

If the men arriving together each Thursday were referred to as the chain, then it made sense to me, a humanist, that the men be viewed as links, as individuals, which they surely became again as those chains were unlocked and collected. They were, of course: I/M Doe, J, #123456, C321–2. Inmate John Doe, number 123456, living unit C, room number 321, bed number 2, or upper bunk.

Their numbers weren't tattooed on their bodies, just on their psyches.

I'd had the chain list since the day before and had reviewed the names and numbers. Names told me nothing: not age, not ethnicity, not criminal background. Numbers told me more. Much more. In Washington state, the Sentencing Reform Act, implemented July 1, 1984, changed how criminal justice operated and how time was meted out. The DOC started issuing six-digit numbers beginning with 9. That number indicates the new guidelines, in which sentences are no longer based on a judge's experience, sense, or whim. Determinate sentencing follows a grid.

The system ran out of 9 numbers by 1990 and started using 7 as the first digit. Most old-guidelines inmates, those sentenced before July 1, 1984, and still in the system or back with violations or new charges, had six digit numbers beginning with 2. Now and then I saw a 1, and once a 0. Someone's grandfather, in the system longer than forever, waiting to die.

There were also men whose inmate number began with 6, which told me they first did time in a Washington state juvenile facility. For some, the system was the only parent they'd known.

The chain is seated now. The sergeant grabs a clipboard with the chain list and calls out the men's last names and numbers.

"Here, here, here . . ." They've been told how to answer: "Yo" and grunts are not acceptable. Their eyes are on the floor, some voices barely audible.

They're given cell and bed assignments, printed rules and regulations, routine orders about where to report next and where they'll get their ish.

Ish. Their state-issued khaki pants and button-front shirts; their underwear and socks, and one red bandana; their watch cap and cheap tennis shoes; their bar of soap, comb or hair pick, and toothbrush. (With the influx of gangs, the institution stopped issuing red bandanas. They have khaki ones now.)

"What about our personal property?" asks an inmate.
"It's on its way," the sergeant says.
"When do we get it?"
"When it gets here."

Their property—the few possessions they've been allowed in prison—is somewhere else. It never arrives with them. In some cases it never arrives. Period. There are always tort claims for lost or stolen property being filed and investigated. A man takes a good leather jacket to prison, or a cashmere sweater, or just a pair of jeans that fit. Something special to wear on visiting day. It disappears.

"When's it expected?" The question is ignored.

"What about the money on our books? That come with us?"

"Listen up," the sergeant says. "I don't want to repeat any of this. Your property gets here when it gets here. Your money gets on your books when it gets on your books. This is how we do things at McNeil Island. We go through the rules with you, we get you assigned, we get the hospital staff in to answer questions, we get you fed. You do as you're told. You go to gym or yard if your unit's called to go. Otherwise, you stay put. I don't want any of you getting written up before you get started. Is that clear?" He waits for nods. "Tomorrow morning and every morning next week you report to the cell house sergeant at 0830 hours for escort to the education floor for orientation. Unit counselor here will tell you more about that. You'll see more of Ms. Walker in orientation. Anybody decides to get out of orientation by messing up and going to the Hole this weekend goes through orientation when he gets back in population. It's mandatory, order of the superintendent. Any questions so far?"

They shake their heads without looking up. It's time for me to leave.

During my years at McNeil, men told me chain day was one of the worst days they experienced. Most wanted to get their state-issued gear and bedding and flop on their bunk. If they were lucky, their cell mates wouldn't hassle them and they could escape into sleep. More than a few said they'd thought about the Big Sleep on chain day.

I climb the stairs from R&D to the main corridor, push the button to summon an officer, and wait to be let out of one secure

area so I can enter another. Lieutenant Burton happens by and un-
locks for me. Or perhaps he's been there, waiting for this moment.

"What did you think?" he asks, his hazel eyes dancing. I always
find those eyes in that brown face intriguing. Whose genes gave him
those eyes? He reads what I thought about seeing the chain go
through their introduction to the island and finds some delight in
my misery. We've become friends—leery friends, I'd say, neither of
us quite certain the other should be trusted. My rational, compas-
sionate arguments butt heads with his rational, tough, law-and-
order arguments.

"It's demeaning, demoralizing. I'm depressed."

He unleashes his deep laugh and one of his clichés. "They didn't
get here by singing too loud in the church choir."

"No, but how they got here is a long story, isn't it? One that
started early in childhood. They all have a life story; they've all inter-
nalized a sense of being bad, no good, worthless . . ."

"Whoa, whoa, whoa, you don't know that."

He's wrong; I do know.

Studies of criminal behavior show the majority of people who
commit the most serious crimes were battered and abused and
internalized self-hatred by the time they were five or six. If they
had had a balance, even one person who saw worth in them, it
might have been enough to keep them from the criminal path.
But too often the battered and abused child acts out his anger and
hurt at school, and "gets in trouble." Again, I'm not saying this to
justify criminal behavior. I'm just offering information. I believe it
should enter into every person's critical thinking. I believe we can
do more to deter crime. My beliefs are not born of a bleeding-
heart liberal teacher's do-gooder confusion. My training and expertise are in child and family studies; my experience is solid and
growing—still growing, even now as I write.

Every man on every chain had a story. Most of them would
rather spend their prison time in solitary confinement than tell.
Things brought to light get into records. When you dance to the

concertina's tune, you don't trust, don't feel, don't tell. Counselors call it the victim shield. The shield has been penetrated in recent years, the stance brought to light by those who do tell. And tell and tell and tell.

But prison is not *Oprah*. Quite often it's a game of charades.

9 A Distinct Link

As part of my determination to treat inmates like students, I made an effort to put names with faces and to learn first names during the first two PSR hours on Monday morning. I observed each chain's arrival for clues to their group dynamic and began making mental notes to pass along to our team when we met at the end of the first two-hour session. It was generally easier to get acquainted with chains of fifteen or fewer men than with those of twenty-five or more.

Chain lists and daily attendance rosters listed inmates by last name, first initial, DOC number, and living unit. Most DOC personnel took attendance with last name and number. It was less time-consuming than asking every man to give his first name, but it was not my style. Some men liked being asked and even smiled as they responded. Some got into their "Who wants to know" or "Who cares" attitude. I cared, and I moved to stand or kneel by desks until I had eye contact. "I want to know your name."

Every chain developed a group personality, some memorable enough to be discussed for weeks. Almost every chain had a few inmates transferred from other prisons because of a change in their custody status and a few new inmates just beginning their sentences. Most large chains had one or two men who acted angry for a few minutes and then relaxed, and one or two who acted bored until they saw our team lineup. At some point during the first two hours when an associate superintendent and the shift lieutenant dropped in to meet them, even the angry and bored sat up straighter and took a second look at the program agenda.

One chain remained fragmented the entire week. They arrived in the bleakness of winter when flu running rampant in the old cell house had reduced staff to a minimum and left me without a TA and without the DOC personnel support that made the program work. I see that as a vital factor for such intense orientation programs in any prison; the number of presenters and their positions matter as much as the content, and the presence of an inmate TA projects the message that inmates living in the institution validate the program. I remember the chain because of specific incidents that interfered with my teaching role and in a sense cast me into an officer's role, and because of my renewed resolve to keep those roles separate. I also remember it as connected to the strong trust many inmates placed in me through the ensuing years.

Eleven unlinked individuals trooped in to the PSR classroom that winter Monday morning, anger seeping from every pore. When I had met them briefly on Friday they had been quiet, spread out. I hoped that meant an easy week, but it wasn't to be. Five of them slumped into chair desks across the back of the room and stretched their legs to block that aisle; two took window-side seats and fixed their gazes on the distance; one sat door-side, fourth row back, head down; one absolute center, hands folded; two front and center, side by side, chairs pulled too close.

Had the shift lieutnenat been there, he might have said, "Actions speak louder than words." He most certainly would have told them to sit up straight and reminded them that they needed to show respect for others if they wished to be treated with respect in turn.

The group included one man with a Hispanic surname, quite obviously one of the two men in the front row. He looked very young. I hoped the man beside him spoke Spanish and was sitting close to help him understand. When Mr. Gomez was present, he sat with the non–English speaking men and gave them verbal and nonverbal clues to help them follow the instruction. I believe he also offered a measure of comfort in a new and strange setting.

We were having a Pacific Northwest day—cold rain, curling fog. Most of the men wore jackets, though their trip from the cell house was a dry one. They were buffered against something else. Why hadn't someone called fog line? (Fog line halts inmate movement to programs and most work stations; beefs up perimeter checks; and gives teachers a little extra time to prepare lessons, grade papers, use the restroom.)

I took a deep breath, introduced myself, and asked the men to answer roll call with their first names. Some did; some grunted to show their disgust with the mandatory program. The Hispanic man, listed as "Diaz," said, "No hablo inglés," and grinned. "Alano," the man beside him said, and placed a protective hand on Alano's arm. The toucher was perhaps ten years older.

I stared at the hand until it moved. We all knew the rules: no touching. I hoped he was there to help clarify what was confusing material for non–English speaking students.

"Do you speak Spanish?" I asked the older man.

He shook his head. "Nope."

I looked at the clock. Eight forty-five. I'd be alone with this group, one of whom would not understand what I said, until 10:30, and again from 12:30 to 2:30. Maybe a plea for help in the 10:30 meeting would bail me out, locate another Spanish-speaking inmate or staff member. Maybe not, with so many out sick.

I distributed folders, paper and pencils, the schedule—all things Mr. Gomez handled—and said, "Our bilingual clerk is on sick call. I'll do the best I can."

"Sheeiit."

My eyes narrowed and held the speaker's—one of the men at the back. "I wouldn't be surprised, I hear it's a nasty flu." He got the message, gave me a belated grin. I smiled back. It did little to ease the tension in the room.

I turned a chair desk around so it faced them and sat. "Okay,

let's hear it. Tell me what other than the usual prison complaints
is bothering you."

The older man said he thought Alano should be excused from
the group since he couldn't understand a word I was saying. I
heard a similar request every week; it opened a door for me.

"I'm not authorized to excuse students, but I will try to find a
translator. You can ask the cell house sergeant when you go back
at 10:30." It wouldn't change anything, but it told them who had
authority in the matter. I scanned the room. "Next?"

Most of the others spoke, several at once. They had places to
go, things to do, jobs to try for. I nodded, restated their gripes with
expletives deleted, a concept I taught in positive parenting classes,
empathized with their frustrations, kept my own to myself. They
got most of it out. It had been a miserable trip from Shelton,
where they'd been held in restricted units too long. An extremely
unpleasant officer had greeted them at the island. They were stuck
in cells with men who snored all night. And farted.

"We been jerked around since Thursday, and we're tired of it,
man."

I nodded again. "I understand, but I'm not the Man, not the
person who can do anything about those concerns. I am a Pierce
College instructor. Coordinating this program and teaching some
of the sessions are my job, and I'm going to give it my best."

While I spoke Alano tore a piece of notebook paper into quarters. I shook my head at him. The man beside him leaned in close
and whispered, "Shh." A gust rattled the windows just then and
men laughed. It had been a loud whisper and seemed responsible
for the window. Laughter helps, but it didn't last.

In the somewhat less strained atmosphere, I introduced the
material on roles and got some discussion going. If the lieutenant
had been there, he would have said it was like pulling hen's teeth.
Alano folded and creased another piece of paper, and another. The
quiet man in the middle of the room, the one I'd deemed a loner,
finally spoke. His voice was soft, difficult to hear over Alano's
creasing and tearing. My blood pressure rose.

Most of the time I avoided using my position of authority in the classroom; I liked my confrontations to be in discussions of controversial material. But the tearing annoyed me, and it wasn't because paper was so difficult to come by. I collected Alano's torn pieces and set them on the lectern.

Finally, period movement. Men tripped over desks in their haste to get outside to smoke. Alano went to the lectern, pointed at his papers. I nodded, and he gathered them and arranged them in a neat stack. The education secretary in charge of supplies, a rather rigid woman with a German accent and a sweet smile, would have a fit if she saw precious notebook paper torn into pieces. She was responsible for our supplies budget, which remained inadequate for our needs. I understood her position and would have purchased a truckload of supplies from my own funds to make her or any other person step into the classroom with me to ease the tensions during the next hour.

She, of course, had a deadline to meet. All the education staff, a resourceful bunch, had deadlines to meet or other places to be. I don't know how they knew that chain was fragmented, unless they read it on my face. I went to my office to make a couple of phone calls to beg someone on the PSR team to give me a hand. No one answered. Word that this chain had problems had spread fast. It began spreading back in Shelton before those men ever chained up for the bus ride. I was on my own.

The old education floor had two long, perpendicular corridors, a security nightmare when only one officer was on post, which was the case many mornings. The officers' desk sat in a recessed area near the top of the stairs, about the middle of the main corridor. That corridor ran from a large learning lab classroom on one end, past a standard library, a law library, and the education staff offices, to the staff restroom on the other end. The other corridor had nine classrooms, my office, an inmate restroom, and an alcove that served as a cramped waiting room where nonsmokers gathered on rainy days.

My office looked out on the alcove. Alano was there with a pencil and his stack of paper, now folded and torn at one corner to keep it together—a tablet of sorts. The older man who sat beside him in PSR was there, and several others I didn't recognize; they were not from the PSR group. Something was going on, going down. The only officer on the floor monitored the stairwell. I opened my office door as a warning to break it up, met wary and smug eyes. All conversation and activity ceased, but the message resonated: you didn't see anything, you don't know anything, you can't do anything about it. The intercom snapped to life, and a voice announced period movement was over. There were shoulder slaps, "see-ya's," as men moved toward classrooms.

In PSR men got seated; I took roll, got a couple more first names, announced how we'd spend the next hour. Alano unzipped his khaki jacket and shrugged it back on his shoulders, an exaggerated feminine gesture complete with adjusting his chest for effect. Under the jacket he wore a state-issue white T-shirt that had odd protrusions. Two odd and lumpy protrusions. Crumpled paper? Not his torn notebook pieces; they were clutched in his hand.

Much as I hate pointing fingers, I pointed at those lumps. "What are those?" I meant it to be rhetorical, to warn him back into his jacket.

"Chessies," Alano said.

Chessies. All eyes were on me. Someone in the back row said, "Lana, call him Lana." Chairs scraped.

That's when I realized the older man beside Alano was acting as his pimp. I should have called him out to the corridor to warn him that such activities would not be permitted in the classroom. Instead, I focused on Alano. "Get rid of them."

"No hablo inglés."

"Bullshit," I said, and watched his eyebrows move up. He had heard that phrase before, and possibly understood more English than he acknowledged. Prison administrators believe immersion in the English-speaking prison culture helps non–English speakers learn the language. Most of the Hispanic men sought prison jobs, which they combined with education in English as a Second Language (ESL) classes.

"That's English slang. Even if you don't understand a word I'm saying you know what I mean. Get rid of them." *Chessies.* The word sounded British or Australian to me, not at all typical prison slang.

Alano reached a hand up under his T-shirt and pulled. Toilet paper came out as streamers. He patted it into mounds alongside his little homemade tablet. I took a closer look. The tablet was his "little black book." Names. Assignations, I supposed. The man beside him surely helped record the names during period movement. That's what was going down in the corridor alcove.

"Put the toilet paper in the wastebasket. Put the notebook paper pieces in your jacket pocket and leave them there."

He curled his mouth down, opened his eyes wide, and held out his arms. He'd watched too much television. "No hablo . . ."

"Now." I pointed at the wastebasket, but kept my eyes on the remaining ten men. Well, nine. The man next to Alano was too close to me, and I now knew where his interests lay. He would collect some of the pay, most likely items from Store, that Alano received for prostituting himself.

Several of the men uttered pejoratives, pervert and queer being the most polite. They knew the relationship between Alano and the other man, and distanced themselves from it by shoving their chairs to the back or far sides of the room.

I thought about my dad, who taught me to buck up and look for reasonable solutions in tough situations, and wondered what he would have advised. I think he would have told me to confront the issue. I asked, "What in addition to homophobia must we overcome to make Social Responsibility bearable this week?" No one answered, so I repeated the question. It used up time, and I was too irritated to teach. Irritated at prison staff, not inmates. Someone on staff in the cell house knew that Alano was what they called a cell house whore; someone should have prepared me for potential repercussions in the classroom.

The man in the middle of the room said, "You need to define homophobia." He didn't mean for himself, and he was right on about the need.

"Homophobia," I said after drawing in and releasing a deep breath, "is a fear of homosexuality. It's very common in heterosexual males. 'Homo' literally means same, though I know it's used as a slang term here; 'phobia' means fear. 'Hetero,' of course, means other, as in other sex." I wrote the words and meanings on the board. We were still working on roles and rules. "One heterosexual male role is to mate with females for sexual purposes, which includes reproduction of the species."

We had an interesting discussion after that, nine of them and I. The man seated next to Alano busied himself with his folder and papers, and didn't look up, and I chose not to make that an issue. As I taught in parenting classes, ignoring undesirable attention-getting behavior when possible often stops the behavior. Once the nine men in the middle and back of the room got started talking, they were quite open about their own sexuality and managed to get in some bragging. They engaged in sexual intercourse only with women and avoided sexual congress with other inmates at all costs. Their vocabulary was a little dicier, but they meant the same thing.

While the discussion progressed, I noticed Alano and the man next to him doodling or drawing pictures on the back of the PSR schedule and on their folders. I glanced at their sketches just long enough to realize they depicted specific sex acts. I needed aspirin. At the very least I needed aspirin.

During the next period movement, before our team meeting, I told the education floor officer about Alano and asked him to check before the afternoon session to be certain he didn't again have "chessies" inside his T-shirt.

"Shim, you mean?" the officer said. "Check the shim. He's a shim, he wants to take it in the butt, that's his problem, not mine. Let him stuff his shirt."

"Not in my classroom." I watched his face, a nice burnished copper face under silver curls. He was a retired military man and would soon retire again, from Corrections. I'd known him as a gentleman who complimented women on their clothes and hair. Mine was silver-white, lighter than his. He called me an ash blonde and generally treated me with respect. I wasn't prepared for "take it in the butt," or his lack of concern for what I considered a predicament.

Education floor correctional officers regularly walked past classrooms to observe inmates' behaviors. That officer had stepped in several times to tell a man who was slumped in his chair to sit up, and more than once to rouse a man who'd dozed off. (I tended to let them doze; those who did were adjusting to heavy medication, and cell house staff had warned me they might drift off.) I suspect his refusal to help me monitor the behavior of Alano and the other man had to do with his own homophobia.

Our PSR team meeting was brief. As part of my responsibility to the team and the program, I described the morning's events, including Alano's use of toilet paper, and the difficulty with getting the class to interact. I was told no one could step in to help me with the afternoon presentation. Every area of the institution was short staffed. Inmate counselors and supervisors went back to the cell house on alert for potential conflicts among the PSR group. The afternoon session dragged; Orwell's "Shooting an Elephant" was a real stretch. I considered staying home the rest of the week, pleading illness, but there was the image of my dad shaking his head. That went against the stoic Norwegian grain. I had to carry on or risk his disapproval. (He'd been dead nearly twenty years by then, but strong family values and a work ethic don't dissolve with a parent's death.)

Before I met the group on Wednesday to teach three hours of parenting and family history, I received messages from education staff, corridor officers, and unit counselors that Alano was gone. All the messages were about the same, but the education floor officer's the most telling.

"Shim's in Seg on a Major, a 504." His laugh thundered down the hall.

Seg: Administrative segregation. The Hole. *Serious Infraction 504: Engaging in sexual acts with others with the exception of spouses during approved extended family visits.*

Had the cell house officers waited for Alano to make his move so they could infract him? Of course they had. Until they caught him in the act, they couldn't stop it. In truth they could never stop it, but they had to make their point now and then.

Alano's removal from PSR eased some of the classroom tension, but it was an unpleasant reminder that the reality of prison life would always interfere with correctional education. The man who acted as Alano's pimp remained quiet and alone. I will never know how much he influenced Alano's decision to stuff his T-shirt with toilet paper, or why he believed I wouldn't challenge such an act.

As PSR coordinator, I did encounter many more challenging individuals: a schizophrenic who needed professional help, not our program; a man with bleeding ulcers whose pleas had been ignored until he vomited blood and spattered other men; several young inmates whose disruptive behaviors were said to be conduct disordered, but whom the system expected to complete PSR before intervention or help was offered; and an increasing number of Asian inmates who understood neither the Spanish-speaking TA nor any of the instructors.

Still, the chain that included Alano Diaz was perhaps the best example of the challenge education and prison staff faced in delivering Project Social Responsibility to inmates. One inmate, one mishandled event, undermined the goals of the program by giving some correctional officers and other staff who enjoyed attacking it the opening they needed. They made the incident into a sexual joke and tried to keep it alive by baiting me and other teachers. The event reinforced a personal rule I'd followed at the women's prison: do not ask officers to intervene with students unless the student's behavior is a threat to others' safety. In seven years at MICC, I had only one potentially dangerous incident, and the education officer appeared in the classroom before I had time to seek help. He'd heard the ruckus, and several inmates had placed themselves between the angry student and me, making it difficult for me to leave the room. Even though I would still tell a man who attempted to look more like a woman by placing protrusions inside his shirt to remove them, I would do so privately. And rather than tell a number of people such as our PSR team about the behavior, I would tell only the inmate's counselor, and let the counselor handle the matter.

10 Families and Other Unusual Formations

We gathered on Wednesday, ten disgruntled inmates and one harried teacher, to peel away layers of resistance, to search deeper for their humanity. We'd come to Wednesday, and the heart of the reason I transferred to McNeil Island: Parenting and Family Education.

As a group they did little to make my task easy. I wrote a formal definition of family on the board: A *group of interdependent persons who share some values and goals, and who are committed to one another over time*. I read it aloud, defined interdependent, asked if the word "committed" bothered them. They shrugged.

"The definition is accurate," I said, dusting chalk from my hands, "but not the only way to define family. Let's hear some others."

Silence. Stares. Shifting in seats.

"I start with that formal definition because it's broad enough to acknowledge prison family groups. Men here—women at Purdy—who bond for the duration of their incarceration are one kind of family for the time they're together."

Dead silence; eyes straight ahead. The women were more open about their prison families: they called other women Mom and even Dad and showed them tremendous respect. Inmates honored with such titles wielded power over those in their family group and often kept younger or more impulsive inmates in line.

"It's quite possible to develop such bonds without their being homosexual in nature."

One nod. Another. Some shuffling.

"Here's another definition of a family, my own." On the board I wrote, "Those persons who walk into my kitchen, open the refrigerator, and complain there's nothing good to eat." The headache that started on Monday and nagged through Tuesday was about to become a full-blown migraine. I wanted a cool, dark room, my bed, utter silence. It seemed I was going to get the utter silence. Our Tuesday PSR presenters said the group was the least communicative they'd encountered since the inception of the program.

Finally one man risked speaking. "What about a dad, a mom, and a couple kids?"

"A traditional family, called the nuclear family by sociologists. A man and woman, and the children born to them."

"Well, maybe to one. Step-kids to the other." The same man, amending his definition.

"A blended family," I said, and wrote "nuclear" and "blended" on the board. In my experience students in any classroom like to see their ideas in writing, and frankly, writing on the board consumed time. They weren't the only ones watching the clock.

"Thank you for responding. Teaching isn't much fun if it's all one-sided."

"Why do you bother?" the man in the middle of the room asked.

"Good question."

Someone snorted.

"Seriously, it is a good question. In my childhood and through college, I swore I'd never teach. But it's in my blood, or in my conditioning from my own family of origin. It's a pattern in my family. My mother was a teacher, and my dad's respect for her dedication to students left a lasting impression."

The man who snorted looked at me with narrowed eyes. "You

know something? You're good. You just threw three words from this list you gave us into your little speech."

"Did I? Which three?"

"Uh, family of origin, and pattern, and . . ."

While he scanned his handout, the man in the middle of the room said, "Conditioning." And he smiled. A smile helped.

"The other reason I teach is ego. I'm here by choice. I believe I have important information to share, and the skill necessary to impart it."

"Yeah, and you don't give up even when you're stuck with a bunch of assholes who don't give a shit. How much you get paid, anyway?"

"This week? Not enough. Last week? Not bad."

One man chuckled; two smiled, then two more. They rearranged their bottoms on the uncomfortable seats. I opened a window, even though it was cold and grey outside. "Let's let some angst escape."

"She said the 'E' word."

"Escape? Whoops, I sure did." The word perks up ears, gives some an adrenaline rush, and sets wheels in motion if spoken in the wrong place at the wrong time. As does the "F" word: Fence.

I'd like to say they became congenial, cooperative students, but it would be untrue. Some groups don't gel regardless of effort. They had been uncomfortable around Alano since they boarded the chain bus, maybe before. They lived in the cell house where Alano and one of his "dates" were busted for engaging in sexual acts. They didn't like him, but disliked the Man even more. They didn't like the old, cold cell house, with its echoes and ghosts (some in the group swore they saw them), men screaming and crying, toilets flushing all night.

One man was doing life without; he'd killed a man a long time ago and would die in prison. He lived through 1970s riots at the state penitentiary in Walla Walla, often referred to as The Walls, or Concrete Mama. He had seen it all.

He started to talk, and the rest of us listened. At one time, when administrators were attempting to implement prison reform, a group of the toughest inmates took over the penitentiary. He'd been in the mess hall when a food fight erupted and became a riot that ended with a death. The Walls was a better place afterward. But he was glad to be at McNeil Island. He preferred the western Washington climate (Walla Walla, in the southeastern part of the state, gets very hot in the summer and very cold in the winter). He liked the MICC views of Puget Sound, sailboats and yachts, ferries and barges carrying everything and everybody to the island, evergreen trees, green hills, deer browsing in the morning and evening.

And then he said something very surprising. "You young guys, you ought to pay attention to the lady here. She's onto something. Any of you got a family out there, you owe them better than doing time. You still got a chance, you do right by them."

The weight of his words settled on those men. I watched for a time, then said, "Thank you. Your message may be the only one any here will remember as the weeks and months go by."

I waited for someone, anyone, to respond, to speak from his own feelings. They were emotionally shut down; they didn't say a word. I sensed the wisest course with them would be personal disclosure in the form of a lecture on family history and patterns. I launched into a story about my family and an old family secret.

"We're going to do a genogram—a graphic picture of family members—using my family of origin. I'll start with my parents' generation. Squares for males, circles for females, the marriage line connecting them, their siblings." I drew a square and a circle on the board for my parents, then twelve more squares and circles on my dad's side, six more on my mother's. My mother had a half-sister, but the genogram didn't show her relationship clearly yet. My parents' generation stretched across the board. The men had a handout explaining the symbols, and they followed it quite well for a group so dedicated to projecting boredom.

"What do you know so far about my parents?"

"They had a lot of brothers and sisters."

I put an X in Dad's square and Mom's circle, and dates below: 1907–1973; 1909–1974.

"They're dead?" one of the men by the window asked. He sounded alarmed, but that could have been projection on my part.

Another, who'd been writing, said, "Not really old. Sixty-six and sixty-five."

"My dad died of a massive heart attack while landing a salmon during a fishing derby. His catch won a hundred silver dollars. My mother, who wanted nothing to do with those heavy coins, or the money in any other form, died of a heart attack nine months later while helping dress my nephew, who was then three years old."

All their eyes left mine to look out the window or at their handouts. They weren't about to let the emotional reality of parents' deaths get too close to their own locked-down feelings.

I went along the board exing out all but one of my dad's siblings, saying, "heart attack, heart attack, heart attack . . . this living uncle had cardiac bypass surgery; this aunt and this one had cancer; this aunt died in her teens . . ."

From behind me I heard, "Lot of heart attacks."

"Yes, a serious pattern of heart disease in Dad's family." We talked then of lifestyle and diet, of the hard physical work my dad and his brothers did, and the hearty meals they ate. Those men advised me to be careful, given my history. I almost swooned at their concern. Still, they didn't disclose anything about their families, nor did I ask them for personal information. A couple were scribbling, a hopeful sign, though they could have been writing letters or drawing explicit pictures of sexual acts. I moved to my mother's side of the genogram, and started the X thing again. Five of the seven had died.

"Some serious alcohol problems on this side of my family," I said, chalk still busy. "My mother's father died when she was a child, before her youngest brother was born. I don't know much about my grandfather, but an older cousin who is daughter of this aunt here [I added my mother's half-sister] believes he drank heavily and got violent when he was drunk."

I let them study the whole picture of my parents' generation and let them think about the problems I'd mentioned, both common problems in families of men who go to prison: alcohol and violence. They looked up at the board, looked down at their hand-out of symbols, looked back. One man said, "The way you drew the half-sister one . . . was she the man's child, and not the woman's?"

"Right," I said. Finally, I had a little interaction, and at least one man paying attention enough to discern what the genogram told them.

"Her mother die? The mother of your half-aunt or whatever she is to you?"

"We thought so, until my mother died and we found some old papers of Grandma's among Mom's things. One of the papers was my grandfather's divorce decree. My mother's youngest brother almost had apoplexy over that news."

"Apple what?"

I laughed. "Apoplexy is an old-fashioned word for stroke. And a favorite word in my family of origin." I wrote the word on the board. "My grandfather's divorce was one of those family secrets . . . the kind of thing children aren't told. Every family has some secrets. This one wasn't so awfully bad, but it upset my mother's youngest brother. He had created an idealistic image of the father he never knew. Divorce didn't fit his picture."

One man nodded, then another. Two men lingered in the classroom during period movement. They wanted more informa-tion, but weren't forthcoming with their own or willing to ask di-rect questions, so we just chatted. I was in my realm, my comfort zone, and their increased interest did more for my throbbing head than any amount of aspirin could. I decided to risk telling them the long version of a family secret I believe is associated with stress-related headaches.

Period movement ended; the men returned to their scattered seats; I took attendance and a deep breath and returned to the board, where I wrote "M" by the symbols for my mother, both my sisters, my oldest son, my only daughter, my only niece, and one nephew.

"Migraine headaches are a pattern I've identified in my family. They began with my mother. I'm working in spite of one right now, not as bad as hers were. Perhaps telling you what I believe is the origin of the pattern will help my headache ease. I hope so. Perhaps it will help you understand the innate power of family history and patterns. I hope that even more."

Their eyes changed, they leaned forward, and they listened with interest. Their attitude changed en masse.

11 Family Patterns and Secrets

By the time I started teaching male felons, I'd honed the self-disclosure method of teaching to a fine art. Students heard about my family's foibles and strengths and had a solid sense of our family history and patterns. They didn't hear names or dwelling locales. I'd used a short version of the following story in classes, at correctional education conferences, and once when demonstrating family history to Department of Corrections personnel developing the family facet of the state's new case management program.

Not every group or class heard all the details of the story as I've written it here, but all knew that it was a family secret that negatively affected a family for three generations. I tempered the telling with a caution:

Children just need to know simple truths. Do not go into details of gory events or emotional crises.

My mother was seven when her dad died, suddenly she'd been told, of an asthma attack. He died at home; she knew nothing more. She had no idea where she was at the time, possibly high in the arms of a madrona tree where she went with her books to hide and read. She loved books and read beyond her age.

Why hadn't someone told her what I'm about to tell you? She

had been there, in the same room with her dad, but she died without this knowledge. She suppressed it, and there it stayed for the remainder of her life. Was it trying to peck its way through her subconscious shell every time she had a migraine? Were those migraines, nearly sixty years of them, related to the heart problems that caused her death?

Why did her sister, my Aunt Stella, tell me this story so graphically some ten years or more after Mom died?

"He died. What difference does it make how he died? He died, and we managed, and here we are," Aunt Stella said in her rather gruff, matter-of-fact way.

Yes, here we are, my two sisters and I, still affected by the death of a grandfather we never knew, through the trauma it inflicted on our mother, who suffered debilitating headaches the rest of her life. They came on when stress built up, and they sent her to bed in a dark room for two or three days at a time, a couple of times a month.

Lars Nelson died in 1916 in his home on Puget Sound, north of Bremerton, in the house he'd built at the turn of the century for his wife, Ida. At the time of his death, he worked in Seattle as a carpenter and commuted by auto ferry to spend weekends with his pregnant wife and their children: sons sixteen, thirteen, and four; daughters ten and seven.

I imagine my grandfather choking, unable to breathe, and panic settling over the household. They're all there, though the four-year-old is napping in a bedroom. Was the north wind howling down the sound, as it often did? Was rain blowing in under the roof of the big front porch? Was Lars drunk? Was he in a rage? Had he spanked a child? My mother perhaps, with a piece of kindling? Or thrown a chunk of firewood at an older child in anger because a chore wasn't done properly in his absence? Had a cow gone unmilked?

What caused *this* asthma attack? What made it worse than others? My aunt doesn't know. She remembers a wheezing sound; she knew her mother was worried. She remembers her older brothers bolted from the house at their mother's orders, spoken in

Swedish. They ran to the beach, dragged the rowboat to the water. Stella watched them row away, side by side on the middle seat, their strength doubled. Then they were out of view, and her dad was slumped in a chair, and her mother was boiling water to make steam to help with the breathing.

"Where was my mother?" I ask.

Aunt Stella shrugs. "Under the kitchen table, with a book, maybe. Or out in the barn sneaking food to a kitten she'd saved from drowning. Who knows?"

There's a long spell of time when calm prevails in the house at the edge of the sound, though my aunt knows her dad isn't doing well. But she's only ten, and not completely aware it isn't just another weekend day when her father's home for a time. In her old age she remembers her father as a wonderful man and is certain he never spanked her, though he may have spanked my mother, who seemed determined to avoid chores. Aunt Stella says my mother always got out of helping in the house. Where, I wonder, did Mom develop her outstanding cooking skills?

"Your dad taught her," says my aunt. I don't protest. My dad could cook.

The boys and the rowboat return with a passenger, a doctor from the naval torpedo station at Keyport, over four miles away. My aunt remembers some scurrying after the doctor came on the scene, and possibly more boiled water. Her father is stretched out on a daybed in the living room. The room is hot, crowded, but quiet. The doctor's in charge now. She thinks he told them to stand back, all except Ida, who is at the doctor's side to assist him. The boys are in the kitchen, probably eating—they were always eating—so she must have been there too, preparing whatever they ate. She has a clear memory of my mother now, in the living room, standing by the door that opens onto stairs up to the bedrooms.

There's an odd noise, then a gasp, a shout, a moan, and a child's scream. My mother's. My aunt recalls the scene as bloody. Blood all over the daybed, and on the doctor's hands, and on the wallpaper. This seems important. The walls have a nice wallpaper, and now it's spattered with blood. The source of the blood and the horror taking place are secondary to her awareness of the damaged walls.

"Then all hell broke loose," my aunt says. "The boys and the doctor ran for the rowboat and rowed off to get more help. Mom sent me up the hill to a neighbor's to get linens. Your mom was screaming and screaming, and banging the stair door against her head. Screaming and banging, and the boys and the doctor going off, and my mother just rubbing and twisting her hands. I remember I didn't run. It was a steep hill."

Maybe she knew it didn't matter: her dad was already dead, though no one had said as much. My aunt remembers returning home with towels and sheets, but doesn't think the neighbor came with her. Still, the house filled with people, or so it seems now, as she remembers.

She says, "There's my dad, all covered with blood. The doctor slit his throat. And there's your mother, still screaming and still pounding the door against her head. I think she had a book in one hand."

Aunt Stella stretches "slit" so I see and feel the knife. I suspect she's feeling it too and using a brash delivery to protect her own emotions.

"Slit Grandfather's throat?" I say. "My mother had a book in her hand?" And I think about what it means. Is my aunt's picture accurate? Does it matter now? Not to our mother, but to my sisters and me, and our children?

"Yeah, slit his throat," Aunt Stella says. "He was trying to do a tracheotomy, the navy doctor, and cut the jugular vein. I guess you'd call it slitting his throat. Blood squirts all over the place when the jugular gets cut."

"The doctor accidentally cut the jugular?"

"I guess you'd call it an accident. I think the doctor might have been drunk."

My aunt says "drunk" like she's spitting out a worm that came with a bite of apple. She dislikes drinking. I know she's seen her share of the damage alcohol does and wonder if she remembers, but denies, her father's being drunk that day. And other days.

I'm back where I started. Was Lars Nelson drunk? Was he in a rage?

Was he? Because I'm in a rage the first time I hear this story. Why didn't someone tell my mother? Why was it important to keep it a secret? Why am I learning this now, long after her death, too late to help her?

My aunt ends the story by saying they ruined a lot of linens, mopping blood. She's not sure just how they prepared the body for burial, or who built the coffin, or how body and coffin were removed from their home to the cemetery. A horse-drawn farm wagon, she thinks.

My grandmother spoke limited English. She had Swedish friends nearby, and I imagine she may have confided a little of her pain and sorrow to them. She had a cousin in Iowa, with whom she corresponded in Swedish, and another in Kristianstad, Sweden. She had five children at home and one on the way. They lived on ten acres, with an apple orchard and milk cows. She was thirty-five years old, widowed, and quite isolated down there on the water, so far from a highway. They managed.

How should her father's death have been explained to my mother in her childhood? How should the family have discussed the event? I'd suggest something like this:

"Your dad had a history of serious asthma problems. He had a very bad attack. A doctor came to the house and performed a tracheotomy [or surgery—wording depends on the age]. It's a dangerous surgery. Your dad died. You were there, and you were very scared. I'm sure you remember the blood. Seeing blood frightens children."

Asthma might have to be explained to a child, though one who'd lived around a person with the disorder would already know enough about it to recognize the word. Once a simple, straightforward explanation has been made, the child should be encouraged to ask questions and express feelings. Traumatic events need to be discussed again and again, and even written about.

I'm writing about it now because I believe it is an important piece in my life's puzzle. Learning of the event enhanced my understanding of how children carry trauma into adulthood. As firstborn daughter, I took on responsibilities for caring for home and family when our mother went to bed with a migraine. Even as a child I could see the migraines coming. Her eyes changed, lost their spark; her entire persona dulled. Within a few hours she would be vomiting and moaning. The vomiting would last an entire day. She spent at least two days in bed, and a third holding her head. I took over her household duties. I often browned a pot roast, made white sauce for macaroni and cheese, or fixed salmon patties from a jar of our home-canned salmon with instructions Mom moaned to me while holding her head. There must have been cookbooks in the house (I have one Mom used, published by Good Housekeeping in 1930), but I don't remember using them for meal preparation. For baking, yes, but not for cooking. There seemed to be a distinction.

Of course, my two sisters and I developed migraine headaches and still suffer them at times, though not with the horrible intensity Mom did. We have the advantage of understanding what stress does to our bodies, and we learned long ago which foods trigger headaches in us. I set out to learn more when my children first experienced them, and began the task of unraveling the pattern.

How did I do this? First, I identified the pattern, and then I determined when and why it developed. In my mother's case, I believe stressful events placed her back in a situation she couldn't handle. Her body must have known the scene needed to be released, examined, explained, but her conscious mind followed the family's unspoken rule. They did not talk about her father's death. Some therapists call family secrets a conspiracy of silence.

Someone's doing, or having done, time in prison is often a family secret. Thus, my mother's story, or more accurately my story of learning the truth she never knew, relates to inmates in an orientation or family program. They need to find ways to help their children, and other family members, hear and cope with the truth of their criminal behaviors, and the resulting incarceration.

They need to search for and examine patterns that influenced and conditioned them, so they can help their children avoid them.

Ten men listened to the long version of my family secret and talked about it back in the blocks. They helped cement my reputation for understanding that bad things happen in families. They arrived in PSR angry to a man and left, as they said, with food for thought. Though I can't prove it, I believe some among them paved the way for the trust men placed in me for the duration of my career.

Trust began with the loner in the middle of the room, the one who told me I'd need to define homophobia. Before the week ended, he found his way to my office to tell me his secret, the one considered most horrible in prison. He was doing time for sexually abusing his stepdaughter. He needed to talk to someone who understood about families, not just about crimes. He was the first of many sex offenders, far too many it sometimes seemed, who needed to talk.

They talked to their classification counselors, and many of them to therapists, as part of the prison drill. They worked on their cases and time structure with their counselors, on issues and strategies with their therapists.

Then they talked to me about their deepest feelings. They knew I didn't repeat their stories to anyone, and I didn't keep recorded accounts of what they said, or how they appeared as they spoke.

Healing requires talking, verbally releasing all the awfulness of one's past actions. I trusted them with a personal story, and they trusted me in turn. I was "real," an important quality with prison inmates.

Being real made me a safe person when they were ready to tell, to feel, to trust. I accepted listening as part of my role and handled it well enough for most of my tenure. Looking back, it seems their truths started bothering me one day and became too much the next, but that wasn't the case. Their stories, coupled with the tough-on-crime legislature's decisions to increase prison time and reduce money spent on education, wore me down until the day I decided it was time to move on, to put my energy into writing. It took four years of writing fiction before I started working on this memoir, and now it's time to write about the truth often called a dirty little secret.

I still find it difficult to comprehend how many children in our society suffer sexual abuse, and how many adults still struggle with the aftermath of such violation. Perhaps the next chapter will shed some light for all of us.

12 Sex Offenders

I did not become inured to criminal acts because I taught criminals. I did not argue any individual's innocence or get on soapboxes on their collective behalf. I did like some students more than others. Any forthcoming teacher at any level would admit as much.

One of my favorite students killed a man who molested his two stepdaughters. He is still doing time for murder.

Another favorite, now out and rebuilding his life, is registered in his community as a sex offender for attempted adult rape.

My fondness for them had nothing to do with their criminal acts. I liked them for all their other characteristics and traits. Both were honest about their lives prior to the commission of their crimes, worked hard to grow beyond those criminal definitions, and showed genuine concern for family members and friends (their own and their victims') hurt in the commission of their acts.

One of the men is an accomplished fine artist whose work is shown and sold in galleries. The other is an artisan with wood. I own, treasure, and display with pride one item created by each.

Both are intelligent, educated, and accomplished in other areas. Both worked as teaching assistants in adult basic education (ABE) classrooms and took every college-level, personal awareness, and vocational class they were permitted by legislative mandate during their incarceration. They spent time in my classroom as students, and as volunteer assistants when my workload overwhelmed me. I remain in touch with both.

At the time they committed their crimes, both were abusing alcohol and other drugs. I offer that as information, not excuse. It is a common factor in the commission of many crimes. At least one former Catholic priest who sexually abused young boys admitted to alcohol addiction and suggested in an interview that other priests guilty of child sexual abuse are also alcoholics.

Why did I care? For two important reasons. First, understanding human nature and motivation is important to me, and even after working with untold numbers of adults who sexually abused children, I still struggle to understand. Second, almost all sex offenders return to their families or start new families. That reality needs to be considered when we make decisions about other offenders. It certainly influenced me, and it influenced my work. I was, and remain, an advocate for children.

Whether committed by male or female, child sexual abuse garners the most severe emotional response from the taxpaying public. We hate it. We are sickened by it. We want such offenders removed from our society. We ignore their need for education and guidance, their own background as victims, their shame and suffering. We want them locked up forever.

But that doesn't happen. I repeat: almost all sex offenders return to their families or start new families. They need help. They must cope with their offenses inside the fence and back outside in our communities.

And so I'll help by writing about what I learned as I worked with those inmates who chose to talk and tried to change.

When Ron, the loner from the fragmented PSR group, told me a chapter of his story, he merely scratched the surface. It took at least a year, and several classes with me, before he related the whole story. I'd sensed he was a child sex offender. To my growing despair, I found I could spot them in a group of offenders. There was an air about them. Remorse? Shame? Possibly, but if those feelings did exist, they were underlined by more telling factors. They tended to distance themselves physically by sitting alone when space permitted, and by making little eye contact with other men in their group. They didn't enter into typical group banter, complain about the expectations placed on them by the prison administration, or resort to nonverbal behavior such as kicking a chair or slapping a folder onto a desk to show their impatience. They didn't fit parameters of prison-wise older offenders or street-wise younger ones. Most were well-groomed; most had high verbal skills and had held successful positions in their communities.

They were typical "guys next door" in middle America.

Ron, the first sex offender at MICC to confide in me, said without preamble, "You couldn't help your mother with the problems that developed in her family, but you've helped me. I'm a sex offender. My stepdaughter's my victim. I've been worrying about keeping that a secret here, and I haven't given much thought to her . . . the rest of my family . . . how they're all hurt . . . what they need to do. I see, now, the danger in secrets."

I remember feeling prickly things climbing my spine and slithering down my arms and thinking, "Dear God, do not reveal your crime in this place; that's not what I meant." I remember saying, "There are professionals here who will help you with your burden. You do know, of course, not to discuss your crime with other inmates."

How's that for a sensitive response? I know I made good eye contact with him, and I must certainly have had a look of empathy on my face, because he met my gaze and tried to smile. His eyes were wet. I think mine must have been hard.

"No," he said. "Oh no, I don't intend to admit to anything beyond problems with alcohol, and an estranged marriage. Guys tend to think domestic violence when they hear your marriage is on the rocks, and I let that ride. It's just that I found a new way to think about some things, and I want to thank you. You've already helped me."

It's always nice to be thanked, especially after such a trying week. Maybe Ron's sense of clarifying his thinking redeemed me a bit. I certainly hadn't helped Alano Diaz, though I'd learned a lesson: be careful when asking for officer intervention with undesirable classroom behavior. I could (and did) handle Alano, but word got around on the prison wireless, and it gave people another reason to attack Project Social Responsibility as a waste of employee time. And now, to cap off the week, I was listening to a man confess to child sexual abuse. I wasn't certain what Ron expected of me, and didn't want to hear specifics of his case. In his defense, he wasn't trying to dump his worries on me: he was simply thanking me and stating the nature of his offense.

The Washington state criminal code specifies sixteen classifications of crimes in the chapter titled "Sex Offenses." They range from rape in the first degree and rape of a child in the first degree to custodial sexual misconduct. They do not include incest offenses, prostitution, or patronizing a juvenile prostitute. Those are classified in chapters titled "Family Offenses," "Indecent Exposure and Prostitution," and "Bribery and Corrupt Influences."

I may have missed other classifications; I'm not trained in the law.

All have the same classification in the prison convict code— "rapo."

Scum, the worst of the worst, fair prey for prison rapists. Especially if they committed child rape or molestation, which makes them "baby rapos" or "baby fuckers."

In other inmates' eyes, Ron was all of the above.

During my tenure at the women's prison, a female dubbed a baby fucker by other inmates was raped vaginally and anally with a mop handle to "teach her a lesson." Does that make sense? They hate the crime, so they duplicate it.

Ron knew he would be subjected to such treatment if the general population learned details of his crime. He was handsome and rather slight of build, an easy mark.

Another among my female students doing time for sex offenses was a woman in her middle years who had several grandchildren. She was called a baby fucker because her husband had sexually abused their daughters and she had known about it but hadn't

stopped him. She wanted to enroll in parenting classes and participate in a parent-cooperative preschool program then meeting inside the fence. Other inmates banded against her, and she accepted it as her lot in life, much as she'd accepted the abuse she
also suffered at her ex-husband's hands. She remained in ABE
courses and longed for an opportunity to learn more about positive
parenting, child development, and family history and patterns.
When I first met her, she made an X beside the signature line on
her school enrollment forms: she couldn't write, let alone print,
her own name. During her incarceration, she earned ABE certificates for learning to read and write and do math; she was there
long enough to get her General Educational Development (GED)
degree, which substitutes for a high school diploma.

Her daughters visited her over the years, and they were ready
to welcome her home to her role as mother and grandmother
when she was released. They forgave her, though not their father.
Her earliest parent education took place as she completed work-
sheets while learning to read and write, and met with me one
on one. She never got past the inmate barrier blocking her from
parenting class and preschool lab participation. That's the
strength of the convict code, even in a small women's prison.

At MICC the PSR team believed confronting inmate attitude
included getting men to examine their view of sex offenders. We
needed to push them to rethink the rapo label, and to speak out
against acts of violence done in the name of cell-house law. That
became part of my presentation, much as it was in parenting or
family history and patterns classes. Men needed accurate information about sex offenders and offenses, and I had completed special
training in that field. Because discussion stirred up such anger, I
kept my presentation academic, beginning with legal issues, statistics, and definitions, and heavily focused on pedophiles and child
molesters.

(Over half of all male offenders then at MICC had references
to attempted adult rape in their presentence investigation reports,
but they were not doing time for sex crimes. The accusers were
generally women with whom the offenders had personal ties.)

Psychologists, sociologists, and criminologists define a pedophile as a person who believes the relationship with the child is romantic, grooms the victim for sexual encounters, and uses charm and threats to keep the encounters "our secret." Pedophiles usually abuse the same victim again and again over an extended period. They may have multiple victims, often siblings or friends in a community group, but they tend to abuse far fewer children than child molesters do.

Child molesters, by contrast, tend to have multiple victims, chosen at random. Molesters rarely victimize the same child more than once. A prosecutor told me it was not uncommon for a molester to have one hundred or more victims a year. A child molester is the unknown "bad man" lurking in the alley or more often the playground.

There is no known "cure" for pedophiles or child molesters, though behavior modification is used with some who fit an "amenable to treatment" profile and who agree to the tenets of treatment. The majority of their victims are female.

I gave groups time to digest the information and didn't interrupt the diatribe that followed. If I were teaching now, the sexual scandal reaching into the Catholic priesthood would present another dimension to discuss. Most of the offending priests were labeled serial pedophiles, and most of their victims were young boys. As you might guess, those homophobic MICC students considered men who sexually abused boys worse than rapos and baby fuckers, and unworthy of life, even in prison.

Where does Ron fit in this picture? Where does his offense register on the criminal justice scale? On the emotional barometer? I'm going to relate Ron's story because it is emblematic of so many men's experiences, and because he and most of the others have returned to society and have not reoffended.

Ron took several classes from me, worked for a time as a TA on the education floor, and met regularly with a DOC psychiatrist. He had been charged with and found guilty of child rape in the second degree, defined in the state statute as "sexual intercourse with another who is at least twelve years old but less than fourteen years old and not married to the perpetrator and the perpetrator is at least thirty-six months older than the victim." The age specifications in the offense are critical: pedophiles and child molesters almost always select much younger victims.

Ron was sentenced to seventy-six months, the mid-range for a first offense in that classification for an offender with no prior criminal record. Had he been charged with incest in the first degree, a crime with similar parameters but classified as a family offense, he could have been sentenced to as little as a year and a day. (The year-and-a-day sentence, or twelve to fourteen months, sends a man to prison rather than just to county jail.) Prosecuting attorneys and the criminal justice system decide case by case whether to charge an offender with a sex offense or a family offense.

Ron felt he'd been unfairly treated by the prosecutor and believed that with professional help he would be able to stay with his family and heal the wounds. He wanted his wife and all the children to have counseling, which they were getting by the time I met him. He hoped their counselor would encourage his wife to remain in the marriage and bring the children who weren't his victims to visit. After all, his wife had been having an affair, which was the reason Ron gave for becoming involved with his stepdaughter: he saw it as getting back at his wife for the hurt she'd caused him.

Ron was a late-stage alcoholic at the time he first sexually violated his stepdaughter. He'd had a couple of DUI (driving under the influence) convictions, though he'd served no jail time for them. He was a successful blue-collar worker with a good income, a nice home, and children who succeeded in school and extracurricular activities; the family were respected members of a church. And then his wife went out and had an affair.

Ron had a knack for downplaying his crime, the sexual abuse of his stepdaughter, to focus on other factors of his life that showed him to be a victim. He'd been through treatment programs for alcoholism and quoted literature that declared alcoholism a disease. He had a disease, his wife had had an affair, and he had found solace elsewhere.

It took Ron a long time to look back at his family of origin and identify the patterns he'd followed. Rather than work to understand the roots of the pattern, he wanted to skip ahead and get his family of procreation to understand. But first he needed to go back. Ron's dad was an alcoholic and was physically abusive. His mother drank, but only socially. I always pointed out the use of qualifiers such as "only." Inmate students often used qualifiers when they talked about their lives and family issues.

Finally, when it became clear Ron's wife wouldn't bring the children to visit, and in fact was filing for divorce, he started telling the rest of the story: the pattern. His mother sexually abused him. She saw him as her little man: her husband was often away from home, or at home but passed out. Ron was a victim of sexual abuse and a child of alcoholics. He started drinking young to ease the pain of the things his mother did to him. He once tried to talk to his grandfather about his mother and was beaten and called a liar.

There's the pattern. Abuse begets abuse begets abuse until someone stops it. Ron knew he needed to face his own role as victim in his family of origin, do his work to find resolution, and then help his family of procreation. He needed to expose the secret and break the pattern; he needed to free his children. He just didn't know how to begin.

His children's counselor helped them, but children heal faster when they know the sexually abusive father understands the harm he's caused and has a sense of why he committed the abuse. They also must hear the abuser say it was not their fault. They needed their dad's permission to talk and heal, and enough history to know he'd entered adulthood, marriage, and fatherhood as a wounded human who brought forth his pain, his family secret, to the new family.

Ron needed to quit being a victim, part of his pattern, so his children could grow healthy. He needed to quit blaming others because it was keeping him a victim. He needed to grieve for the hurt done him, and I urged him to do so. But my role as parent educator was to teach parents what children need and how to help them achieve those needs.

I liked Ron and willingly listened to him when he wanted to talk about his life, but I also expected him to work with a therapist. He was a good student, grasped concepts including family-system theory, and continued to reach out to his children. Their relationships mended; his stepdaughter was able to confront him, with her counselor's help, and then to forgive him. Ron, with his therapist's help, accepted that.

Ron's mother was still alive. She continued to be his biggest stumbling block. He couldn't get her to admit she'd ever done anything to hurt him or any of her children. She was the perfect martyr—the wife of an abusive, alcoholic man and a mother devoted to her children—and the only thanks she got in her older years was a bunch of messed-up kids. She had complaints about all of her children, but of course Ron disappointed her the most. It's not easy to have a son in prison for a sex crime: the whole world reads about it in the paper. (Ron said it never made the news, so far as he knew. He lived in the greater Seattle area, where most crimes don't get newspaper space.) Ron's mother was a victim who used blame as a shield.

It should come as no surprise that the grandfather who beat Ron and called him a liar had sexually abused Ron's mother through most of her adolescence. Did the abuse go back further? If so, that information is buried with Ron's grandfather.

There is one family's pattern of a dirty little secret: sex abuse. In some families it takes incarceration to break the pattern. Families whose incarcerated member learns enough to help the rest of them are fortunate.

When Ron left prison, he registered as a sex offender with the police department in the community where he settled, but no one posted negative flyers about him. The likelihood he will reoffend is very low.

Over the years, I met and worked with several dozen men with stories so similar to Ron's they seemed to be reruns. They were nice-looking, well-groomed men, most of them white, who had grown up in financially stable families; attended good schools; married relatively young; established themselves in successful careers; attended church at least somewhat regularly; and drunk socially at parties with friends or after work with buddies. They had nice-looking wives who also worked outside the home. Most wives had a child by a previous relationship, not always a marriage. Somewhere along the line, as the marriage relationship faltered, the drinking got heavier, and the man slipped into serious alcoholism. He functioned in the workplace well enough to stay employed. He functioned less well in the home.

Those inmates were neither child molesters nor true pedophiles. They were generally responsible men who sought education and counseling. Many worked as teaching assistants in basic education programs, where they helped students with math, reading, and English course work. In time many of them went on to prison construction jobs and sent money home to their families. Some had wives and children who visited; some were able to remain in touch with their children only by mail and occasional telephone calls. Completing parent-education courses was part of their case management plan, and often part of a court order. Those men were sex offenders.

They were sex offenders who would return to their families. They would register as sex offenders with their local police departments, report to their community corrections officers, seek and find jobs, and reintegrate into society.

I worked with them without judging them, pushing them to learn all they could about parenting before they returned home. I taught all who came to me, whether they enrolled in a course or sent a kite (an appointment request) to the education floor because they thought I might be able to help them with a problem or get them some information. I taught them from 1990 to 1997, when parent education was eliminated from the curriculum by the legislature.

One of the most important things I taught them was how to explain their crime and incarceration to their children: how to unravel secrets and tell their children the truth. Telling the truth wasn't easy for them, or teaching them how for me, but I kept at it for their children.

Long before the legislature declared parent education at Mc-Neil Island to be a frill that could be handled by volunteers, there were detractors who maligned me for the tax dollars spent to educate Ron and others with similar crimes. I said to them, "Would you rather they not be educated?" I say it still, when in fact much less is being done.

13 Tell the Truth

Tell the truth, but not the gory details. Tell the truth, but don't admit to or discuss your sex crimes inside the prison fence. Tell the simple truth. As I listened to myself, I heard the dissonance: truth is rarely simple.

Our culture values truth. My edition of Bartlett's *Familiar Quotations* lists 220 "truth" quotes, and another 26 about "truths." Children are encouraged, or ordered, by parents and other adults to tell the truth. Witnesses in court raise their right hands and swear to tell the truth, the whole truth, and nothing but the truth. Still, we read or hear news accounts of persons lying under oath.

My mother accused me of embroidering the truth to improve a story, which I do when I want to entertain or make a point. Yet, as I write this memoir, I avoid some truths about former students' crimes because their inclusion would serve only as gratuitous shock, when my purpose is to examine the worth of an unusual career.

When I said "Tell the simple truth" to a group of PSR inmates, thought wheels whirred. Which truth? The one they denied, diluted, plea-bargained down to the least-possible prison time? The one they still can't face themselves? That truth?

I dropped "simple," a poor qualifier, which left the value-weighted word "truth." The concept worked well with students enrolled in Positive Parenting, which included a unit on dealing with children who lie, cheat, or steal. Those students, enrolled in a class to learn parenting techniques, could approach the information as parents, not criminals. I needed a different approach for the other students and went back to basic rights and responsibilities, the subtitle of my book *Parenting from a Distance*.

"It's your right and responsibility to tell your children where you are, and why," I said to a new PSR group during the parenting and family session. The anxiety level in the room shot up. I felt it and smelled it, like a fetid odor carried on a changing wind. I heard and saw it: chairs scraped; eyes turned toward windows or desktops.

I'd worked with women who found creative ways to avoid telling their children about prison, who diluted their truths and mitigated their responsibilities, and who remained involved in their children's lives. Most incarcerated women I taught had been the primary parent before being arrested, had better verbal skills than male inmate fathers, and handled emotional matters with more ease. Some of that had to do with sex-role conditioning, some with sex differences. I considered those factors and tailored my approach to fit male strengths, offering them three sentences that cut to the chase.

I broke an adult rule (or law). Prison is my consequence. It's not your fault.

The explanation looks good on paper or the blackboard, but it doesn't roll off the tongue with ease for several reasons. The first sentence requires the parent to take responsibility right up front. "I broke an adult rule." That doesn't fit advice parents who are also convicted felons receive from defense attorneys.

I'd give my little lecture on telling the truth and hear, "Wait a minute; I'm not copping to anything."

And, "Consequence? Who the hell talks like that?"

"Me," I said. "My children, who learned my tricks, and suggested 'consequences' when they knew they had to face them. My students, who get beyond those value-weighted words 'good' and 'bad,' as in, 'That's a good girl,' or 'You're a bad boy.'"

Bad boy, hah! Most of those men had grown up with abusive, derogatory language, often delivered with a physical exclamation point—a swat, slap, arm jerk, or worse—and were so unaccustomed to appropriate verbal discipline they sneered at my three sentences. They'd used parenting methods their parents used on them, methods "necessary" to keep children in line.

"And it succeeded with you in your childhood?" I asked, and watched their nonverbal response. "You're in a prison classroom, talking to a parent educator, and supporting what I consider abusive or neglectful child rearing." I'd get some half-grins, odd grunts, averted eyes. "You grouse about punitive treatment by correctional officers and the system, and yet you justify such actions by parents?"

It got their attention. Of course, I explained that it's human nature for us to defend parents and practices that were the norm in our childhoods. They needed to consider alternatives, to learn or relearn appropriate disciplinary methods, and to choose for themselves. I knew that inmate students, almost to a person, suffered horrible guilt for something they'd said or done to a child. They needed to forgive themselves and move on; they needed to work on strengthening their parent-child relationships.

Some children knew the truth about prison because the parent was arrested in front of them, or the crime occurred in their presence. Some knew because they were victims, as in cases of child abuse or child sexual abuse. Even in those cases, the child needed to hear the parent say those three things:

I broke an adult rule. Prison (jail) is my consequence. It's not your fault.

Many male felons considered it easier to tell a child, "I did something bad," than to say, "I broke an adult rule." Stimulating discussions led most of them to find a "good" way to explain their crime and incarceration to their children. In the end I was less concerned about the wording than the communication.

A successful discussion, especially one in which students could argue a bit and hear me concede they were the ones who knew best how to talk to their children, got them thinking and learning. I wanted to provide information and suggestions, not an absolute solution. And I liked the energy of those arguments. It created a healthy learning atmosphere for all of us. It led to my next favorite statement:

"Separate deeds from doers. 'I did something bad,' not 'I am bad.'"

They liked that. "Hey, Mom, I'm an okay dude, I just did something bad."

I soon learned that the men in PSR who beat their chests the hardest bragging about their misdeeds and who clung most tenaciously to the convict code were the ones who would stop me in the corridor to ask questions or send me kites to request a private meeting. They wanted their children, nieces and nephews, parents, other relatives, or friends to see them as people, not just criminals, but couldn't risk showing their need in class. I understood and told them so.

During one PSR session, a biker with huge tattooed biceps (he'd had to open the seams of his state-issued T-shirt sleeves to accommodate them) came up at period movement and shoved a blank piece of paper at me.

"Write that stuff down. The explanation stuff. Not the 'It's not your fault' part. I got that okay. The rest of it. The 'deeds and doers' stuff. I'm a doer, you know what I'm saying, but I got a couple kids out there, and I don't want them to end up in prison."

"Sure, Mr. Johnson," I said, and smiled up at him. On first roll call he'd told me to call him Mad Man. I'd given him my left-eyebrow-raised look and settled for Mr. Johnson. His DOC number indicated he'd been around the system for a while, and he had an image to uphold. He had long hair, an unkempt beard, and dark-circled, hard eyes. He stood too close, but I wouldn't back up. Maybe he, like me, was myopic.

"I've got other materials I can give you, if you're interested."

He looked at me with such mistrust it made holding my pen

steady enough to write the deeds and doers stuff, as he called it, a serious challenge. But write I did.

"Do you want other materials?" I asked, as I handed back his paper.

"You know something, you've got a nice smile."

"Thank you," I said, and kept smiling, though I wanted to put space between us. When you teach, you go with what works.

"What ages are your children?" I wanted to stay in teacher mode.

"One's eleven, one's almost fifteen."

I think his eyes softened. Or maybe that was magical thinking on my part. "Would you like me to photocopy some information about explanations for preteens and teens?"

"Yeah, but don't make it a big deal. Just hand it to me, okay?"

"Okay, if you promise me one thing."

He pulled his head back, but kept his feet planted. "Yeah? What?"

"When you tell your children about doing time, be honest about how sad it has made you."

It took him ten seconds to answer. My mouth went coppery. Dry and coppery.

"Yeah, okay, you say so, I'll tell 'em." He took the paper and lumbered out the door. The remainder of the week he stayed in the classroom through period movement when I was there, which told me he wanted to talk. A smoker's passing up a break was a sign something was going on. I went to him, sat in the chair desk next to him, and initiated conversations with him. All who observed, and many did, saw me make the move, not him. He taught me some truths about bikers' lives. I urged him not to romanticize the life to his children, especially not the criminal expectations placed on certain biker gangs to earn the pins some wear on their leather jackets. He gave me one nod. I don't know if he rode with an outlaw biker gang, or rode alone as a latter-day cowboy. It didn't matter. He wanted to do something right for his children.

"Kids know I'm in prison," he said. "Me and my old lady are straight up about that. I'm sending her them papers you gave me.

She's doing her job; she's the mom. I talk to the kids on the phone."

"Keep calling them. It helps them know you, and you them. It's more important than most people realize." We both smiled. He liked hearing he was doing something right. I suspected he might not be able to read and comprehend the items I'd photocopied. Students with adequate reading skills often struggled with comprehension if they had damaged their brains with drugs. My colleagues who taught basic skills talked of teaching the same math or English concepts over and over. A student seemed to grasp it during the lesson, but would forget it the next day. I looked at Mr. Johnson's eyes, tried to read what he needed from me, and took a stab at his concerns.

"Children in their preteens and teens tend to get caught up in two major worries about parents. Some fear they won't live up to their parents' successes. Some worry they will repeat their parents' mistakes. Keep telling your children you trust them to make better choices than you made."

He nodded again and handed me his pencil. "Write that down."

I wrote and talked, trying to cram it all in. "Keep explanations simple. Simple works better for all of us. Simple and honest. And tell them every time you make any progress in any area in prison. If you work, tell them what you're learning and doing. If you attend school, send them some of your work. If you enjoy music, write or talk on the phone about what you like. Try to learn what TV programs they watch so you can discuss them. And ask your children what they think about current shows, movies, music, even political matters."

He kept nodding. His eyes changed; something internal was changing. A teacher who sees such change, especially in an inmate student who is a little intimidating, feels thanked and rewarded. I never saw him after PSR week, but I would bet he kept doing all he could to help his children cope with his incarceration. After all, he was a doer, you know what I'm saying?

Many children don't know the truth about an incarcerated parent's whereabouts. They think Mom's going to school in California, Dad's working construction in Florida. Creative inmates set up lies about where they are and why they can't come home. They keep the lies going, getting in deeper, until they have no news to write the child, nothing to say on the phone, and communication doesn't work at all. Or as with one former student, the children visit but are told prison is a hospital, the parent ill.

Sally was doing time at the women's prison when it was called Purdy Treatment Center for Women and programming included outings with community sponsors to swim at the high school pool, ride horseback, even shop at a major mall in Tacoma. The prison was new, the population small. Over 60 percent of the offenders were doing time for property crimes; they weren't much danger to the community. Sally walked away from an outing: she escaped. Prison officials did not like that. It made them look incompetent.

Sally remained on escape status for several years. She married and had two sons, and by her accounts fretted continually about being found someday, arrested in front of her children, and hauled away in shackles. She and her husband talked with an attorney, and Sally turned herself in. She was returned to Purdy and placed in the maximum-security unit (Max), where she spent twenty-three hours a day locked in a single-person cell with a "modern" toilet-sink fixture. She and her husband told their sons she was sick and in the hospital.

Sally registered for a parenting class. She had to do most assignments on her own, though I was permitted to meet with her once a week to go over her work. I stood in the corridor of the administrative segregation side of Max and communicated with her through the cell's tray door, about waist high on me. I squatted or bent over on my side of the door; she did the same on her side.

When her husband and sons visited, which they did most weekends, Sally was transferred to a maximum-security visiting room with thick glass windows and phones. She wore orange coveralls. Visiting time was limited, and there was no physical contact. (Most prison visiting is less restrictive.) She and her husband and sons "touched" while they talked by putting their hands on their respective sides of the window. You've seen it enacted on TV or in a movie. The boys were five and three; holding the heavy black phone receiver tired the younger boy.

I urged Sally to tell her boys the truth. She said she couldn't. How could they understand?

That was the first time I pushed my three simple sentences. I recited them.

"That sounds phony."

"A lie is better?"

"I can't tell my sons I'm in prison, I just can't. They'd never forgive me."

"What message are your boys getting about hospitals? About your health? They come here, wait for electronic doors to open to let them inside a fence with razor wire stretched along it, walk through a device that sounds alarms if their shoes have metal supports in them, wait for another locked door to open, and another, and yet another. The hospital staff here all wear blue uniforms with walkie-talkie radios dangling in leather cases from their hips. How do those look to a child?"

It took her a long time to decide, but finally she told them just as we'd practiced. "This isn't really a hospital; it's a prison. I broke a rule a long long time ago, way before I met your daddy, way way before you were born, and I have to live here a while longer as my punishment. I love you both." Tears streamed down her face and fell on the shelf where her phone rested, as she waited for the shock of the truth to settle. Her husband was there to console the boys; at least they had him on their side of the window.

Her five-year-old son said, "Oh, Mom, I'm so glad they finally told you. It was hard to pretend."

She sobbed for days afterward over the burden her older son had carried. He had known but hadn't talked about it to his dad, his grandparents, his younger brother, or his friends. He assumed the role so often shouldered by firstborns: he kept a secret to protect those he loved.

Another woman who created an interesting but untrue story for her child was a federal inmate transferred to Washington state in a move to reduce overcrowding at the federal prison at Pleasanton, California. Such transferees were generally stressed by the transfer, but Carla tried to take it in stride. She'd been enrolled in a good education program there and wanted to continue working toward a college degree.

Carla was doing time for delivery of controlled substances and mourning her husband's death. He was a bush pilot who went down in his plane somewhere in Florida. She'd been involved in his drug deals and received a rather lengthy sentence. Her parents, in another southern state, accepted custody of Carla's four-year-old daughter and agreed to do all they could to help mother and child remain in touch.

Carla wrote her daughter creative letters and illustrated stories. She made cards and inexpensive gifts in a program we called parenting lab and mailed them with lovely little notes. She talked to her daughter weekly about going to school and what she was learning. The phone calls were paid for by her parents. Carla's daughter believed her mother was in college somewhere far away.

One Sunday, while they talked on the phone, her daughter said, "I'm never going to college. College is mean. They won't let little girls visit their mommies."

Carla wept as she told her story. Women could cry in class in the 1980s and be comforted by their peers. Rose, one comforter, had regular extended-family visits with her children. They spent two days together in a trailer inside the prison fence, romped in the yard by the trailer, played board games, read books, prepared meals, watched television, and talked about worries and joys. She talked to them on the phone between visits, told them about her classes and school work, and asked about theirs. They talked about serious things and silly things. They communicated.

Carla's parents said they would bring her daughter for such a visit if she chose to tell the truth. She wanted her parents to do the telling and then bring the child. Her parents, already burdened by her life choices, gently said no. It was Carla's responsibility.

They would pay for the phone call, no matter how long it lasted, and they would comfort Carla's daughter afterward.

Carla wrote out what she'd say and asked me to read it—a handwritten document ten legal-pad pages long that detailed the drug running from Colombia to Florida and all the ruses and dodges they had used to make the trip work. It said nothing about breaking laws. I found it fascinating. Carla bit off her fingernails while she waited for my response.

"Shred it," I said.

"I won't remember what to say. I need to read it on the phone."

"Okay, take a clean piece of paper and start with the simple explanation we discussed in class: 'I broke an adult rule called a law. Sometimes, when adults break rules, they go to jail or prison. I am in a prison. I go to a special school inside prison.'"

She wrote. We practiced pausing for her child to ask questions. She was certain her daughter would ask, "What rule?" Most children do, and the parent needs to be ready to answer honestly without terrifying a child. Carla could answer she sold drugs but did not use them. When we finished practicing, Carla said, "Should I send this?" She waved the legal pad. "Or just keep it for when I see her? For future reference, so to speak?"

"Do you want it read by the officer who examines mail before it goes out?"

"No!"

"Do you want it with your personal items during a shake-down?" (Officers are trained to watch for such items.)

"No, you know I don't." She picked at her fingers, looked out the window, everywhere but at me. "It's a lot to tear up and flush. And that's a major." (Inmates often got rid of unwanted items, including notes, by flushing them down the toilet.)

"How about shredding it?"

We went together to the school office, a place out of bounds for inmates. Carla felt uncomfortable. Staff conversations ceased. I explained we had a little project. Carla did the shredding; staff members watched and wondered why I didn't just shred the pages for her. It was important for Carla to do it herself for two reasons: she knew they were shredded, and she symbolically ended the justification of an illegal act.

"Okay," she said when we left the office, "I'm ready to face the music."

Later Carla told the parenting class her conversation with her daughter had gone quite well. Of course her daughter forgave her; she was only four, and she so needed her mother that anything could be forgiven. Their relationship began to change, Carla said. They talked about fibs and lies, and telling the truth. At four, children are learning about identity and power in relationships, and they need parents who are secure in their own identity and who can provide accurate information about the child's world.

Carla told the truth and kept it simple.

14 Cope with Consequences

Consequence. The word inmates didn't like. They preferred *punishment.* I unraveled that with students in classes and informal discussions and came to the same conclusion every time. Punishment is inflicted on a person by an outside force; it's beyond personal control; it permits the punished to blame others for their incarceration. Consequence implies that personal choice led to the circumstance. That's heavy, man.

As a parent educator, I urged students to *discipline* their children rather than punish them, a fine-line distinction, considering each verb is included in the other's list of synonyms. Discipline by my definition meant to teach, train, or correct. My MICC students accepted it as other-inflicted. They went to disciplinary hearings where a disciplinary officer read the infraction written against them and issued a decision. They might lose earned time or good time, or be given a sanction, defined in Webster's dictionary as that which induces observance of law. The prison system hopes sanctions teach. Inmates see sanctions as punishment.

Comparing prison infractions, disciplinary hearings, and sanctions to parenting helped me teach that negative consequences result from misbehavior. At the time I taught men at McNeil Island, there were twenty-nine possible minor infractions or misbehaviors. They included unauthorized possession of stamps, theft of food, abusive language, refusing to obey an order, smoking where prohibited, and unexcused absence from any assignment. They're not too far removed from misbehaviors parents cope with daily.

The sanctions imposed for such infractions included loss of yard or gym time and added living-unit chores. They're similar to what a frustrated parent might choose as a consequence for a child's misbehavior. They're far more reasonable than the serious abuse many students had experienced at the hands of a parent when they were caught with an unpermitted item, when they sassed or cussed or refused to do as told, when they were caught smoking or skipping school.

Eighty-eight serious or major infractions resulted in more serious consequences, just as more serious misbehavior within the family requires more stringent measures. For instance, Alano Diaz of the "chessies" went to the Hole for his serious infraction.

Whether they called incarceration their consequence or punishment, many men thought being sent to prison was easier to handle than explaining prison and their crime to their children. One man I'll call Luke said, "Prison as a consequence is easy. I did the crime; this is my consequence. Telling my little girl what I did is the hard part."

His crime couldn't be argued away or made more acceptable by substituting another word. It was truth time: time to explain the adult rule or law he broke. Time to talk about choices and actions, and the consequences that reach beyond prison into families of victims and victimizers and change them forever. Luke's daughter knew he was in prison, and she wanted to know why. "Why can't you come home, Daddy? What rule did you break?"

Luke took every course I taught and talked openly from the time he came through Project Social Responsibility about his father role and his worries. Luke was in his late twenties when he was transferred to McNeil Island and had done several years for murder. He had recently married a childhood sweetheart who had a daughter by a man who left before the child was born. To the child, Luke was Daddy, the only daddy she knew, and she wanted him to come home. She was four, bright, inquisitive, and a tad impatient. She didn't like the early morning trip to catch the bus that transported visitors to the MICC boat, the boat ride itself, or the long walk on the island. Luke said she whined at visiting and continually asked why he had to stay behind when she and Mommy left.

Luke's blond good looks made staff ask, "What's he doing here?" He was athletic, well-groomed, personable, and polite to staff and inmates, and he was an academic high-achiever. He followed prison rules without grousing, picked teachers' brains, and delighted the librarians in his quest for good literature. What could he possibly be doing in prison?

The answer is Luke was doing much the same thing Mr. Johnson, the biker, was doing: learning to cope with a long sentence.

For its part, the DOC supports and permits inmate visits with family members and friends from the community because visiting fosters family unity, makes inmates more manageable, and eases their transition back to society. All visitors must be approved in advance, be on the inmate's visitor list, and abide by the institution's policies. Like most prisons, McNeil Island has a designated visiting room and specific visiting hours.

Though the DOC and individual prisons work to make the process dignified and orderly, there are always problems and complaints from inmates and visitors. Luke's daughter wasn't unusual. To visit MICC, visitors must first register at the DOC bus depot, located on the grounds of a state hospital approximately two miles from the ferry dock. There they board buses for transport to the waterfront, walk from bus to ferry, and wait in line for a personal check-in that includes a trip through a metal detector. Most women visitors carry clear plastic purses or clutches so an officer can easily see the items they're bringing inside. They must have one piece of picture identification and may have unopened cigarettes and matches, up to ten dollars in cash, and limited specific personal hygiene items for themselves and their children.

Some bus and boat schedules have changed since my tenure;

times may differ now, but they will give you an idea of the process. Visiting hours were 9:30 A.M. to 2:30 P.M. five days a week, with most visits taking place on weekends and holidays. Registration at the visitor parking area began at 7:20 A.M., the boat departed at 8:40, and it arrived at McNeil Island at 9:00. The walk to the visiting area and check-in there consumed most of the half-hour until visiting officially started.

Think about Luke's four-year-old daughter's day, and you will understand why she whined. Her mother wanted to check in at visitor parking before 8:00 A.M. to ensure they would make the 8:40 boat, so they left their Tacoma home before 7:30. By the time the child saw her daddy, she'd spent two hours traveling and waiting, looking up at men and women in uniform, and listening to their sometimes impatient comments or commands. At lunchtime, her daddy and other inmates were served a sack lunch; she and her mother, and other visitors, had to buy food from vending machines. (Inmates were not to give their food to their visitors, but most I knew did, and many officers let it go.)

Inmates tended to get caught up in their own preparations for and expectations of visits and forgot what their visitors had to endure just to get to the visiting room. Some inmates didn't like my reminders of the ease of their morning on visiting day. Their breakfast was prepared; all they had to do was walk from their living unit to the dining hall. The rest of the morning was theirs to fill as they wished until they heard their name called to walk to visiting. Now and then one would ask, "Whose side you on?" I always answered, "The visitors' side, especially the children's."

Luke appreciated all his wife and daughter went through to visit, but his daughter's whining was becoming a major problem. He practiced positive parenting suggestions, which included reminding his daughter to use her regular voice and ignoring annoying behavior when he could. He knew he needed to do more. He needed to answer her questions about why he had to live in prison and not at home. Though he was reluctant, he tried the simple-truth approach I taught. When he said he'd broken an adult rule and prison was his consequence, his daughter said, "Say you're sorry, Daddy. Say you're way way way sorry, and you won't ever do it again. Then you can come home."

Luke found me first thing on a Monday morning after his Saturday visit. "Okay, Teach, now what?"

We'd had discussions in class about the importance of using proper crime classifications, being matter-of-fact, and avoiding gory details. We'd even practiced some answers. Luke had tried saying "murder" and given up, had tried "homicide," and had found it too unrealistic for a child. He said no way was the "M" or even the "H" word going to pass his lips. Why, he asked, should children have to learn such words?

Why indeed? Most children don't need to learn them, but they hear them somewhere. Inmates' children often overhear them, or are mocked with them.

Luke sent home class assignments so his wife could study the material along with him. They talked about discipline and problem solving on the phone. His wife started using "time out" on their daughter, always explaining it was a consequence and what misbehavior earned it. Soon that precocious child asked, "How long does my daddy have to stay in time out?" He knew he had to do something more to help her cope with his incarceration and asked me if I'd listen to the story of his crime to help him find a reasonable explanation.

Luke grew up in a small town. His parents divorced about the time he started high school; his dad moved to another state, and his mom started dating. Luke admitted he felt abandoned, though he hadn't used that word at the time. He said he got caught up in some rebellious behavior, but soon learned his mother's threats to send him to his dad were just that—empty threats. His dad settled into a new life and soon called only on Luke's birthday and major holidays.

Luke started roaming at night with a group of kids who had similar broken-family backgrounds. They formed a gang, though it wasn't as sophisticated as inner-city gangs and had no affiliation beyond the city limits of their farm community. Their gang was "into finding adults who would buy them beer and smokes." Now and then they did a little "five-finger" shopping, stealing chewing tobacco, candy bars, sodas; and now and then they got caught and had to work off the value of what they stole. Luke's mom knew he was "getting into trouble" and warned him again and again she'd send him to his dad. In retrospect, Luke said he wished someone had imposed a more stringent consequence.

"Here's how we'd work it," Luke said. "We'd get our hands on some money, some of it guilt or payoff money from our moms or their so-called boyfriends so we could eat out and catch a movie. Instead, we'd pool resources and find a guy willing to pick up beer or cheap wine . . . whatever, long as we had the price plus a little profit for the buyer. There were older guys around who got their own six-packs from profits they made buying for underage guys. We'd drink fast and go looking for a fight. Any fight would do. We were all angry at the world. I'm not blaming my mom and dad, but I know it wasn't a good scene for any of us. Dad's gone, Mom's dating and sometimes having dates sleep over." He studied the desktop for a time. "I know, from experience, how important both dads and moms are to kids."

One night, shortly after his graduation from high school, Luke and some of his buddies picked a fight with Mexicans who had migrated to the area for farmwork. Both sides got into name-calling, pushing, rather typical Saturday night stuff. "We rumbled, man. Fought over some guy's girlfriend. Battered each other with empty bottles and sticks and rocks. In the end we were all losers. Bruised and cut from broken glass. Guys on both sides needed stitches and casts. And one of their guys was dead, though we didn't even know that until the cops got there and got most of us rounded up. One kid on our side said I'd delivered the deathblow. Maybe I did, maybe I didn't. Either way, here I am. I was the oldest one on our side. Just turned nineteen. I'd been warned by cops more than once to clean up my act. In hindsight, I'd say the cops should have locked me up sooner. The kid who gave me up was only fourteen. He went to juvie. He's out now, having a life. No way am I telling any of that to my little girl."

A muscle at the corner of one eye twitched. Luke wanted to cry.

I agreed he should find another way to tell her the story. As she grew, she'd need to hear specifics, but at four she needed a simpler explanation. I watched Luke struggle with his emotions and reminded him, as gently as I could, that children of inmates often look up old police reports when they reach maturity. His head shot up. He hadn't thought of that.

"Let's try reducing the story you told me to its basic elements. Something a four-year-old can understand, but without painting the same kind of scene. Something like this: 'When I was nineteen years old, my friends and I got into a fight with some other kids. People got hurt. One boy died. When there's a death, the prison sentence is very long.'"

Luke thought. The eye muscle twitched. "I wouldn't have to say the M word."

"I think you will have to say it, eventually, if you were convicted of murder—or even of manslaughter."

"Murder two," he said. "I got just under fifteen years; I qualify for earned time and work release." (Sentencing laws at the time of Luke's crime permitted him to earn one-third off his sentence and to do the last several months in a camp. Those laws have since become much more restrictive.)

The weight of it, the reality of his sentence and telling his daughter the truth, suddenly seemed too much for Luke. He dropped his head, hid his face behind his hands. "Oh, God, how can I tell her anything? I don't know, I don't know." We were in my office, with the door closed, but a large window permitted officers and others to look in. He had his back to the window but remained aware of it. He didn't want to be seen or heard crying.

After a time I asked Luke what his wife wanted him to do. They were working together to parent, and her need and opinion were an integral part of his decision.

"She wants our daughter to know the truth, but she wants me to do the hard part. She says I have to tell, and then she'll take it from there."

"What do you want to happen?"

Luke looked up, and a little grin softened his face. "I want you to come to visiting. I want you to handle it. You can make it all better."

"We all want a mother, at times. Responsibility isn't easy."

A primordial groan came up from Luke's depths, as he realized he'd be explaining his crime to his daughter and future children through all their developmental stages. I'd seen it happen with other inmate parents as they reexamined their choices through the eyes of those they love and have hurt. For me it was heart wrenching to witness such pain and to come to terms with the whole picture. In Luke's case, another family, a transient family far from their homeland, had to cope with death.

Luke wrote out and practiced what he would say to his daughter. Thinking about it made him sick to his stomach. He reported he'd thrown up a couple times. He ran the track when he could get to the yard and said running helped; maybe the endorphins flooding his brain let him forget the task he had ahead, and the pain he'd left behind.

Luke must have been the first man on the education floor the Monday morning after he told his daughter about his crime. "Here's how it worked. She was sitting on my lap, and I told her I had a sad story to tell her, and it was a hard one for me to tell. Then I said it like we practiced. The fight, and people got hurt, and one person died. And she pulled away and gave me a look that broke my heart, and she said, 'No, Daddy.' I said, 'Yes, that is what happened,' and I started to cry. She put her arms around my neck, and she said, 'It's okay, Daddy, don't cry. I still love you, and Mommy loves you. But it's very bad to fight. Is that why they won't let you come home?'"

Tears came to Luke's eyes while he talked. Still, he felt pleased with the visit, relieved he'd opened the door to honest discussions of his crime and incarceration. He told his daughter how old she'd be when he finally got to go home. If all went well, if his time wasn't changed by changing laws for violent crime, he'd be placed in a lower-custody institution in two years. His daughter would be in school by then. His wife and daughter had moved from Walla Walla to Tacoma, over 250 miles, when he was transferred, and he envisioned them always moving to be near him, but that wasn't realistic. His wife had a job she liked, a church group that supported her, a place in her community. His daughter attended preschool and had friends.

Luke was working on a college degree and had a growing interest in human behavior. He knew telling a four-year-old child about his crime was just one step on a long climb: a simple explanation for a four-year-old wouldn't suffice as she approached adolescence and developed mature thinking and reasoning skills. He started to look at his family patterns: how his parents had treated him during a traumatic time in their own lives, how he had handled what felt like abandonment when his father moved. Though they had made some poor choices, his parents had continued to provide for his physical needs. Luke had ignored offers of support from within his high school and community; he had chosen behaviors he knew to be wrong. He hopes someday he can help steer at least one child away from the line he stepped over.

The consequences of Kenneth's crime, second-degree child abuse, will live with him in a more immediate way than those of many who were sentenced to far more time. Assault of a child in the second degree assumes the act was intentional and the bodily harm greater than transient physical pain or minor temporary marks. Kenneth had "lost it" with his infant son and violently shaken the baby to stop his "out-of-control" crying.

His firstborn son suffered brain damage from shaken-baby syndrome.

Kenneth was sentenced to three years and court-ordered to complete parenting classes. I first met him in Project Social Responsibility, where he stood out because of his height and his impatience to get started fulfilling the court order. He said he would be permitted supervised visits with his son as soon as he enrolled in a class. A Child Protective Services caseworker would accompany his wife and child to the MICC visiting room for special visits. (Two midweek days were reserved for professional rather than personal visits. Legal, social services, and community-placement interviews were among those classified as professional.) He was eager to start learning. I had to stop him from talking openly about his crime, especially in PSR. Child abusers are often victimized in prison.

Kenneth and his wife married young. She had been pregnant—not an unusual circumstance. Neither his parents nor hers were thrilled about the marriage; both had wanted their children to complete college first. Kenneth was a high school All-American athlete, with the clean-cut good looks of such young men. His wife, a pretty, soft-spoken woman, had admired his athletic ability but didn't participate in sports herself. She had an uncomfortable pregnancy, and then a fussy baby. The caseworker told me neither set of new grandparents was much help to the young couple.

Kenneth said, "I did it. I shook my son and hurt him, and I want to spend my life making it up to him. I just want to do my time and get out and take care of him."

"How will you do that?" I asked.

"Take care of him forever. Do things for him forever."

"How does that help him grow and develop? How will he learn to cope with the learning disabilities the psychologists project? How will he learn to be, and do, and think?"

Kenneth's head hung, and I had a lump in my throat. He was the age of one of my children. My challenge was to teach him the realities of parenting a child who would struggle with learning, with structure and identity, with sexuality and responsibility.

In addition to PSR, I taught six parenting or family-related college-level courses, which were rotated over a four-quarter year. Some were five-credit classes. I couldn't teach every class every quarter and manage all my PSR responsibilities, but Kenneth wanted them all at once. He was determined to learn and succeed. No wonder he'd made All-American. Students like Kenneth can consume a teacher. I had to slow him down, convince him he needed to take one or two classes at a time. Even with one year off his three-year sentence for earned early release, and credit for jail time served, he could fit in all six classes as they were offered.

I joined Kenneth, his wife and son, and the caseworker at their special visits on two occasions, and I stayed in touch with the caseworker by phone. She held high hopes for the child's progress because the marriage remained strong in spite of remarkable odds against it. Kenneth and his wife drew on their faith and accepted support from a church family. She and the child attended special parent/child classes in the community, and he had a former employer who would find a place for him when he got out.

Kenneth had made a horrible mistake, but he wasn't a horrible person. For him prison served a purpose: it was his penance. He needed to do time to grow beyond the quagmire of guilt to the purposefulness of responsibility. Rather than get bogged down in shame and suffering, he used guilt as a springboard to learning. I knew he would never quit suffering and believed others would benefit from all he'd learned. He vowed to become active in helping parents and children when he was released, and he started a community project, with the support of his wife and church, while he was still inside.

Not all those I taught, especially not all those who went through PSR, chose to tell their children the truth about their crimes. Some didn't have the chance: the children heard it elsewhere, or the courts terminated parental rights, which ended the parent-child relationship. Some, especially those who had committed heinous crimes while "drugged out," simply could not find a way to explain what they themselves didn't understand. For those, I suggested saying to their children, "I can't talk about it; I can only say it's not your fault, and I'm very sorry." In many of those cases, the children were, or had been, in therapy because of the crime, and they had responsible adults helping them cope with the consequences of their birth parents' choices.

And not all I taught chose to listen or learn, or to change how they parented. A woman I'll call Tanya took one court-ordered positive parenting class from me in the late 1980s. She was pregnant at the time, and she had other children in foster care. She was a difficult student who argued vehemently that black children must be spanked; according to Tanya, my "white ways" wouldn't work in black families. She turned a deaf ear to reason, logic, replicated research information, and other students, including other African Americans in the class.

Tanya's youngest child, a girl born while she was incarcerated, was returned to her custody after her release. Tanya spanked the child for wetting and soiling, a method of potty training she considered appropriate for a black child. Shortly after regaining custody of her, Tanya spanked her two-year-old daughter to death.

It remains the most heart-wrenching case of my career.

15 Begin with Trust

Trust. It's one of the first and most important tasks of human development. A newborn cries or fusses and is tended to by loving and trustworthy caregivers. When properly formed in the first months of life, trust lays a foundation for all the developmental tasks that follow.

Trust is essential in all relationships and interactions. I relied on a trust bond to grow, teacher to student, student to teacher, as part of my work. In my eighteen-year career, I encountered two students (one female, one male) who rejected everything I taught as worthless; discredited every textbook and source of information as unreliable; and saw child psychologists, social workers, and related professionals as conspirators in a scheme to destroy humanity. It is destructive to have such a student in class. I still hear Tanya in my head.

"Who says? Maybe for your white ways but not for blacks. All that stuff was written by whites who never asked blacks about their children."

I didn't ignore Tanya's concern. Cultural differences must be taken into account in all teaching, especially in the social sciences and human relationships fields. So must stark realities of individuals' lives before prison, possible mental illness left unidentified and untreated, and the aftermath of long-term drug abuse. I sought ways to connect with Tanya because she was court-ordered to complete a parenting class I was contracted to teach.

Tanya had babies without fathers. When she enrolled in parenting class, she was pregnant for a fourth time, uncertain who impregnated her, uncertain who'd fathered her other three children, and unconcerned. They were her children, not some man's; she wanted them back, and she would fight the system to get them returned to her custody. All three children were in foster homes: Tanya did not have a relative deemed capable of caring for them while she did her time. (The system prefers placing children with relatives if possible and helps them qualify as foster parents so they can receive welfare funds.)

In those years, the welfare system did little to connect responsibility for pregnancy to males. Relatives were sought only in the mother's extended family. That has since changed. Women seeking welfare support for their children now must name the father(s), and blood tests are ordered to determine paternity if a woman names more than one possible dad for a child.

Did Tanya want her children returned so she could nurture them, provide for them, protect them from evils she saw in the welfare system? The criminal justice system? Or did she, as one Child Protective Services employee suggested, just want the welfare money?

Men treated women like Tanya as sperm receptacles. Maybe they didn't know they'd impregnated a woman, not for certain, but they wondered. They lived in the same neighborhoods, saw those women's bodies changing, saw them with babies. I listened to women in prison tell their stories. Those men came back around to beg, borrow, or steal the proceeds of those women's welfare checks; to take liberties with those women's bodies; to sleep in their apartments or houses.

I listened to a few men in prison tell the same stories, with a different slant. "The bitch owed me my share of the welfare check, man; the kid was mine too." Of course, I confronted such thinking with facts about the purpose of welfare and discussions of moral and personal responsibility, integrity, and children's need to know birth parents, but the child-as-property mind-set is difficult to change in a few brief encounters. Most who used it avoided parenting classes, and me, until the system started pursuing fathers and enforcing child-support laws. Then, as court-ordered blood tests found them in prison and the Office of Support Enforcement began demanding child support payments, they came to me with their paperwork. They heard I helped dads complete forms to keep their support obligation at a minimum during incarceration. (I'd met men whose accrued debts were so high they said they'd just get new social security numbers to avoid the debt, and then get new families, too.) I gave them a generous serving of information while we completed their paperwork. Many came back for more: a parenting class, open-door sessions, another personal lecture, help writing a letter to a child they'd been identified as fathering.

In Tanya's case, there was no attempt to locate fathers. Her "fatherless children" were to be returned to her one at a time once she was released from confinement as part of her parole plan, a common one for mothers whose children were declared dependent and placed in the care and custody of the state. There were rarely enough foster care homes available to meet the demand; returning children to a mother who had met basic requirements of the law was standard procedure. But Tanya's older children didn't want to leave their foster home, where they felt loved and knew what was expected of them. There they experienced a healthy balance of nurture and structure, the elements necessary for trust to develop, and which thus permit the child to grow through ensuing stages. The Social Services caseworker responsible for Tanya's children opted to reunite her with her youngest child first, and then return the other children as Tanya demonstrated her ability to resume her parent role.

Tanya's daughter had been placed with a foster mother within hours of her birth. The infant bonded with a woman who looked, smelled, felt, and acted nothing like Tanya. The infant accomplished her earliest developmental tasks, including trust, with a foster mother who loved her, cared for her, and kept her safe well into her toddlerhood. Her foster mother was an experienced caregiver. A caseworker representing the state took the little girl from the home and mother with whom she had bonded and formed a healthy attachment, and gave her to her birth mother.

The transition from foster mother to birth mother was disastrous. Tanya, who so mistrusted the world, lacked the skills necessary to cope with the demands of a very young child she'd never known. It might have been easier for Tanya and the infant if she had been reunited with the oldest child first, and then the others in order of birth, but since the children had resisted, the easiest remedy to meet the intent of the law was to start with the youngest child. The decision was a tragedy in the making. Word came down from within the Social Services ranks that someone lost a job, or was demoted, as an internal reminder that repeating such a mistake would not be tolerated.

Reportedly Tanya and her daughter engaged in a power struggle from the beginning. I wonder still how the little girl coped with swats and spankings for misdeeds that are part of a toddler's development. How did potty training become the focal point of their struggle? How many times had the child been spanked for wetting or soiling before the battle that culminated with the defiant child's pulling off her pants and wetting and pooping on the floor right in front of her mother? I imagine Tanya's rage, not just at the mess that had to be cleaned up, but at the child's stubbornness. Tanya told authorities she spanked the child to teach her a lesson. Just spanked. Spanked until the child was comatose. Then, in a panic, she took the child to a hospital emergency room, left her, and ran away.

Over the years I taught men, many argued that spanking a child is necessary to teach the child right from wrong, just as Tanya had argued. I explained the state law for physical discipline, which gives parents permission to use an open hand below the waist, and asked if by "spanking" they meant a swat on a diapered bottom to get a child's attention.

No, they meant sending the child out to cut the switch. They meant laying the child across a bed and laying a belt across the child. They meant slaps, hits, and punches like those they had received from parents they thought had done a pretty good job with them (never mind that they were now in prison). They believed the laws exaggerated the threat to children and sent parents to prison if they so much as swatted a child.

I listened, let them state their beliefs because it's important for all to be heard, and then said, "Not true. It takes more than a little swat for the law to intervene. As a parent educator, I believe even a little swat is unnecessary; a swat teaches children it's okay to hit when you're angry."

Of course, those men never hit a child because they were angry. They hit because the child needed to learn how to behave.

I'd look at them, grown men, most of them tall and broad of shoulder, and ask how they could raise a hand or fist and hit a child of seven or four, or an infant or toddler, when they weren't angry. How?

Heads lowered. They couldn't. It wasn't really about spanking, but about parental rights. Parents often see children as extensions of themselves and the family as sacrosanct and private, outside the law. But laws to protect children have been enacted because children have been beaten to death by parents, and there was the rub. Child abuse is not okay with inmates. Once, in the heat of a discussion on spanking, a man stood, pulled up his shirt, showed the scars on his back, and said, "My old man did this to teach me a lesson, and look where it got me. This sure as hell wasn't a spanking."

Group after PSR group argued about spanking, with men taking both sides, but those who supported it were always a bit more vehement than those who didn't. We moved on, agreeing we all needed to decide whether spanking is discipline that teaches desirable behavior, or release for a parent's frustrations.

How did Tanya define spanking? In parenting class she insisted she meant swats on the bottom, maybe the legs. By then no others in her class agreed. All had at least swatted a child; many of them had been beaten as children to teach them a lesson. They wanted to succeed at using consequences for misbehavior and other methods of discipline that didn't require physical force. Still, they all suspected they would swat a bottom again in life, when they got out.

Tanya got out. I'm sure she swatted, but her daughter did not die of swats: her daughter was battered and bruised from head to feet.

A prosecuting attorney subpoenaed me in Tanya's case. Her defense attorney, a public defender, didn't want me there and tried to block my testimony. I contradicted what he considered Tanya's strongest justification for her actions: she didn't know any better.

"No one ever told Tanya spanking was wrong," he said. "No one taught her how to discipline."

It was a weak defense, but how could anyone find a reasonable excuse for such an event? The female prosecuting attorney, a mother of young children, spoke with me only briefly prior to my testimony. It seemed to take her forever to ask if I had directly addressed the issue of spanking with Tanya. When I finally got to answer, to say yes, Tanya's attorney attacked the course materials and my credentials.

The court and both attorneys had subpoenaed my course curriculum and grade book and had copied them. Prosecutor and defender batted my curriculum and teaching methods back and forth, with me there as observer, unable to speak unless directed to by the judge. Tanya's defense attorney belabored the fact that I'd written the material, suggesting it had no foundation in fact and interrupting my explanation that it was material used nationwide in parent education programs, but adapted to prison circumstances. In the real world, or free world, parents practiced what they learned on a daily basis. Prison mothers had to practice theories of positive parenting in the classroom and through communication they were permitted with their children. Personal and extended family visits provided opportunities to use what they'd learned, and even telephone calls and letters gave mothers a chance to change how they responded to their children's behaviors, questions, and needs. But Tanya had not participated in such interactions with any of her children.

I found myself explaining and defending what I taught to a judge who would decide Tanya's fate and in so doing also render judgment on me, my work, and the worth of prison education. Tanya glared at me. The judge banged his gavel when the defense attorney interrupted my answers. When they finished with me, I was excused to return to work.

By then I had enough experience in courtrooms to expect the veil of sadness that dropped over me after I testified. Though I usually went to court for the defense side, to speak for a child's need for some level of ongoing contact with a birth parent, the immediate aftermath remained the same. I was excused, the next witness called. Someone would let me know the judge's decision when it was rendered.

The judge found Tanya guilty of murder in the second degree; the act was not premeditated. Though she didn't intend to kill her child, she did knowingly beat the child, and the act caused death. Tanya added to her culpability by taking flight to avoid arrest and thereby delaying emergency services for her child. Her prior felony convictions, added to her offender score, increased her sentence to fifteen years. She returned to the women's prison, to the maximum-security unit.

Prison authorities assured me I would not encounter Tanya, even when I went into Max to teach, as if that would somehow allay any personal pain lingering over the child's death and ease my professional responsibilities. She was held for a time in Administrative Segregation for her own safety because of inmates' reactions to crimes against children, but she soon crossed the prison campus with other escorted Max inmates for meals in the dining room. I saw her often and endured her glares and barbed comments.

During the months the Tanya drama played out, I was arguing, and planning, for a program inside the women's prison that would enable inmate mothers and their babies to remain together for a time. New York state had such a program, and other women's prisons worked toward similar goals. A mother-child bonding program, I believe, could have given Tanya a chance to learn parenting methods beneficial to all her children, prevented the tragedy of her young daughter's death, and served society far better financially and emotionally than the existing system.

Further, I believe there were places in Tanya's life where tax dollars invested in her long incarceration could have been spent on intervention. Someone must have known about her life. Tanya had been spanked in her childhood. Beaten with a belt for her own good. Hit up the side of the head to knock some sense into her. Told, repeatedly, how no-good and worthless she was. She lived up to the expectations of the adults in her world. No-good, worthless Tanya got into trouble with drugs and related street crime activities early in her youth, got pregnant more than once in her teens. She parented much as she'd been parented.

Such patterns, such learned behaviors, are difficult to overcome without help. Learned behavior is not an excuse for choosing to commit crimes, and certainly not a defense for violent behavior. Rather, it is a facet of a person's life. Tanya's case was one of many that pushed me to delve deeper into family systems theory, the psychology of the child, and the psychology of the criminal mind. All theories come back to the reality of choices. At some point the person who commits a crime chooses to do so.

In my research I found many felons' childhoods were filled with ruts and holes. Still, many people with such backgrounds do not break society's laws. Stories abound of individuals who rise above the abuse and neglect they experience to become successful members of their communities. What makes the difference?

I believe early childhood education programs, and early intervention with children and youth who exhibit inappropriate behavior, do and will reduce tragedies such as Tanya's daughter's death. While early childhood education is becoming the norm in many communities, other intervention programs are frequently under attack. They are costly and have no success guarantees. The alternative—housing troubled children and adolescents in detention centers—is also costly, and the outcomes predictable. Most will reoffend and do time in an adult facility.

I remain an advocate for prison programs designed to help inmate parents improve their parenting skills before they return to their families. Nationwide, 80 percent of female felons have children, most were primary caregivers before going to prison, and most will resume their roles as mothers.

Because many young women are pregnant at the time they enter prison, I continue to advocate for mother-infant bonding programs inside the prison fence. Washington state's women's prison now permits newborns to remain with their incarcerated mothers for up to eighteen months and to transition with them to prerelease or work release. To qualify, women must have no more than forty-two months left to serve at the time of the child's birth. Mothers and children live in a special unit in the prison, and the children make visits into the community with family members and friends to experience life outside the fence.

Other states have similar programs, though at this writing Washington's is the only one that provides for mother and child to move together from prison to pre- or work release. There are no longitudinal studies yet available, no proof that children fare better. For those who would argue such programs are too expensive, I say, think about Tanya's daughter, dead at age two.

16 Inmates Reparenting Themselves

As I write, I wonder if Tanya's views changed as she did her time. Did she enroll in other classes? Did she find a sense of worth in a prison classroom or job? Are her children getting the care and guidance they need so they will be able to nurture the next generation?

By the 1980s, when Tanya was doing time for drug-related crimes and still considered capable of fulfilling her mother role, family system theory had found its way to the popular press. Our culture had been through two decades of family-fracturing events and had adopted the term *dysfunctional family*. Extensive work was being done with adults who had grown up in alcoholic and other drug-addicted families, suffered divorce of their parents, or survived other abuse or neglect. The reparenting concept was born.

The concept has known several names, some of them considered suspect by academic and political hard-liners. Nurture your inner child, grow up again, heal the child within, and reparent yourself are among the more common terms. All are based on an awareness most of us experience in adulthood when we realize we missed something we needed to make our lives rewarding, fulfilling, satisfying—something to help us achieve a goal or complete the person we intended to become back when we dreamed big and perhaps boasted a bit about our future.

Before you dismiss that as part of the reality of adulthood and say "Grow up" to those who lament what they missed without showing appreciation for what they received, take time to consider the tenets of a basic reparenting program. When meshed with positive parenting, so parent and children grow together, its strengths are clear. To my mind, the best work in the field appears in the book *Growing Up Again: Parenting Ourselves, Parenting Our Children*, by Jean Illsley Clarke and Connie Dawson. Rather than dysfunctional family, they use the term *uneven parenting*. I found it vital in my work with inmate parents. For the duration of Project Social Responsibility at McNeil Island, every man received a "Reparenting for Self-Growth" handout with simple suggestions for self-care while in prison.

Not all parents of inmates had abused their children as Tanya had been abused. A more common story among inmates centered on absent parents: physically absent parents, who left their children behind to fend for themselves; mentally absent parents, who had children because their bodies were capable of reproduction; chemically absent parents, lost in alcohol or controlled substance use; emotionally absent parents, caught up in their own lives and uninterested in children's needs.

Anna, one of my first Family Relationships students in my earliest months at the women's prison, didn't know her father, and her mother fit all four absent parent categories. "I won't live to see twenty-five," Anna said. "I just won't. I know it in my bones."

Though I urged her to avoid such negative thought, to use her intelligence to climb up out of the miasma of her mother's life, Anna said she had started too far down. "My mother's a hooker. My dad was a trick gone wrong. She got pregnant. She did drugs before they were the in thing . . . before the sixties. I remember she slept most of the day. When I was old enough for school, and nagged for clothes and lunch money, she started shooting me up in the morning to keep me quiet. I was a heroin addict at age six, a prostitute not much later. I'm worn out."

I remember Anna as a pretty woman with dark hair and big eyes, a bright though undereducated woman sadly resigned to what she considered fate. She was in prison for a rash of petty crimes committed to support her insatiable drug habit. She earned a GED, applied for education grants, enrolled in a community college before her release, and left prison drug free. She hugged other inmates and some staff good-bye and went back to her world. Several months later, Anna's picture was in the area's major newspapers as yet another murder victim of a then unknown person dubbed the Green River Killer.

In the ensuing years, another five former inmate students were found dead, presumed victims of the same killer, who preyed mostly on prostitutes working the streets near Seattle-Tacoma International Airport. Most victims' remains were found along the Green River, which begins on the slopes of Mount Rainier and empties into Puget Sound south of Seattle.

With the help of new DNA technology, a suspect, Gary Leon Ridgway, was arrested in late 2001, almost twenty years after the first body was found. He had long been a suspect but had evaded arrest. He had even passed a polygraph. In April 2003, when he was facing aggravated first-degree murder charges in seven women's deaths, Ridgway began bargaining for his life. He confessed to murdering forty-four identified and four unidentified victims, and he worked with Green River Task Force detectives to lead them to disposal sites. In exchange, the King County prosecutor did not seek the death sentence in those forty-eight murders.

I turned on my TV set on the November 2003 morning that Ridgway pleaded his guilt in court. The judge read forty-eight confessions Ridgway had prepared, and asked if they were true. The screen displayed photos of the forty-four known victims, one at a time. I saw Anna's picture displayed and heard Ridgway admit to her murder. I heard other things he said: he hated prostitutes and set out to kill as many as he could; he lost count of how many women he killed, perhaps sixty or more; he stopped killing for a time when detectives seemed to be drawing too close to him.

Ridgway was sentenced to life without possibility of parole

for the forty-eight confessed murders committed in King County. Officials in two other Washington counties and in Portland, Oregon, want to talk to him about unsolved murders in their areas. He could still face a death sentence if convicted outside King County.

Anna's story influenced my work to develop curriculum for the prison population. In a sense, Anna spoke to inmate students for the remainder of my career. I told PSR students Anna's story as they glanced at the reparenting handout. A student could choose to think about Anna, rather than himself, as a candidate for reparenting if he wished. The handout began with the first developmental task: trust.

Trust. The word that sends old cons and young, streetwise offenders into orbit.

"Trust who? I trust me. Ain't nobody else gonna see to me."

I heard those words so often I can still picture the delivery. Head forward, forefinger jabbing chest, eyes squinted, hair short or long, combed or wild, or no hair at all.

"I'm a loner, I been seein' to me all my life, I'll keep seein' to me."

To which I'd respond, "You saw yourself into prison," and listen to a string of expletives.

I considered it part of my responsibility to let them express themselves, and if four-letter words were the best they could do, I listened. Keep in mind, they were listening to me too, or they wouldn't have bothered to get so riled up. When necessary, I gave them some four-letter words in return.

Once I had their attention, I explained trust develops when basic needs are met. They were responsible for their own basic physical, mental, emotional, and spiritual needs. They were the ones living inside the fence; they had to care for themselves.

Their thinking ran something like this:

Physical's easy. Get out to the yard or into the gym every time you can. Work out, man. Get on the weight pile, run track, shoot some hoops, swing the bat . . .

Mental's not too difficult. Take a class, watch educational TV . . .

Spiritual, well there's chapel services . . .

With some help, they could even expand the spiritual realm beyond religion. They watched deer browsing, an eagle overhead, a blue heron feeding at low tide, sea gulls drifting on air currents. They looked through the fence to Puget Sound, Mount Rainier, and evergreen trees. There were flowers on the grounds, and almost always in the PSR classroom. They liked to touch and smell flowers, though many did so surreptitiously.

As for emotions, hey, you put them away, leave them behind when you fall.

I pointed out how inmates with trust issues often expect others (parents, teachers, prison staff) to see to their needs, without acknowledging the needs exist. Somewhere in our discussion we got to human touch, and how it relates to trust. Many of those male felons had avoided it altogether. Some had been caught up in compulsive touching; more than a few had a history of joyless sexual touching.

So many of those men who were loners and proud of it became quiet, watchful, when I talked about touch. Someone often said, "Hey, that's a touchy subject." While they were in the throes of considering emotional needs and touch-centered issues, I mentioned skin hunger and what we know from studying data on infants who fail to thrive. Skin hunger is simply the need to feel human touch. Without it, the infant may wither and die. When those men heard specifics of research and learned that most neonatal hospitals and clinics have programs where volunteers hold, touch, and rock infants who are confined for a time, they began to understand the need. It was okay, of course, for those poor little infants, but not for adults. Male adults.

My age (early fifties), my appearance, and something about my general nature helped me pull off the reparenting part of the PSR program with old cons and new offenders, and even many for whom English was a second language. Mexican men got it more readily than others. They rubbed their own arms, patted their faces, and said, "Sí." I appreciated their openness. In some groups, other men followed their example.

We moved on to other child and adolescent behaviors that suggested problems with development. Now and then men would nod, frown, mutter.

Feeling bored, being a bully, using anger to cover fear, abusing power, having to be part of a gang . . . the list is long, and the list of reparenting suggestions is equally long and includes little things men can do in prison without making it a big deal.

Sometimes I repeated a clue. "Having to be part of a gang," I'd say, when the PSR group had young guys trying to keep their power alive while inside, dressed in khaki everything. They flashed their signs across the room, or just to themselves, to stay out there, on top of things while they were down. One young man couldn't believe cell phones weren't permitted in prison. He could not remember being in a classroom without one since age fourteen or so.

"Me and my homies," he began, and launched into a lament that perfectly illustrated how being part of a gang enabled him to *be* at all. I made it a lesson. He wanted to hate me but loved the attention, and he dropped by my office or classroom for weeks afterward to say, "Hi, Ms. Walker, howya doin' today?"

In time he brought me copies of his schoolwork successes, which were at about fifth-grade level. "My homies, they be waitin' for me," he said, and stood by my desk while I glanced through his papers. He was learning and doing what is generally accomplished by children from six to twelve years of age as part of developing internal structure.

"Look how well you're doing. You'll be way ahead of your homies when you get out. You'll need to get them back into school." I planted little seeds whenever and wherever I had a chance.

Reparenting involves learning, thinking, and trying new things, even unknown foods, which men claimed were part of their daily diet. Complaining about prison food is part of the culture, but few skipped meals. In fact, most inmates gain weight inside, where they get three meals a day, medical and dental care, and access to store, where they can buy sodas, chips, candy, and assorted canteen-type foods.

A wealth of help existed for those who chose to work on reparenting. Every teacher and most of the work crew supervisors served multiple roles for those in their classes or employ. All taught far more than subject matter or job skill: they modeled self-discipline and self-confidence and encouraged inmates to grow in both those areas. The shift lieutenant with his pointing finger; a sergeant and corrections officer team who worked with the men on cell-house conflict resolution; supervisors, program coordinators, counselors, hospital staff, and chaplains—all made themselves available to those men.

Many men moved into jobs they earned by being trustworthy. Inmates worked the passenger ferries that carried personnel, inmates, and visitors to and from the islands, and the tugs loaded with supplies needed to operate the facility. They drove buses that transported work crews and staff between the main facility and the Annex. They helped with construction and maintenance and took pride in work done well. They grew up again, often without giving it a thought.

At the end of the PSR week, when we recapped, I reminded them of the resources available, the positive influences in a negative environment. "Eat a balanced diet even if you gripe about the food. Go to yard as often as you can, and while you're out there look at your surroundings. Take advantage of religious services, health services, group counseling sessions, hobby shop. And most of all, enroll in education." (Of course I pitched education. I believe it is the doorway out of prison.) "Most teachers here are so in tune with life, they can answer questions you don't know how to ask."

And one day, when I said that, a young black man with his hair in cornrows lingered. "I gots a question I knows how to axe. You be knowin' Tanya, right? From when you taught the womens?"

"No, I don't recall anyone named Tanya, and I don't discuss students, former or present."

"I knows you be knowin' her 'cause she done tole me 'bout you." His body swayed and dipped while he spoke his street lingo. I'd bet he could do the electric slide with ease and grace. He could

have been Tanya's brother, the dead child's father, another relative, a former boyfriend, a current prison pen pal. His eyes and the
way he stood too close for normal casual conversation told me he
wanted to put me on the defensive.

I narrowed my eyes, studied his, and did what he called a
change-up. "What's your personal view on spanking?" He knew
how I felt.

"Huh?" he said. "Why we be talkin' 'bout that?"

"Why are you choosing to use poor grammar in an education
department?"

"I ain't." He grinned, dipped, did a little soft shoe. Yes, he
could dance. "I just wanted to know . . . do you know her?"

"Same answer as before. I don't talk about students."

"Okay, okay, so you know her but you ain't . . . aren't talking.
I knows . . . know her too, see, and she was messed up on drugs.
Somebody else messed up when they gave that baby back to her,
you see what I'm saying?"

I waited a beat, two beats, thinking about my answer. He had
some connection to Tanya, and some lingering interest in what
happened. Denial of my involvement wouldn't resolve what bothered him. "I do know something about her case, and I do see, and
hear, what you're saying. If it's any comfort to you, Child Protective Services investigated the decision to return the baby before
the older children. I expect they will be more careful in the future."

I watched him try to decide whether to trust me and warned
him off. "If you supplied her with drugs at any time, I'd rather not
know. If you're the dead child's father, I'm sorry, and I urge you
to enroll in a parenting class."

He shook his head, swept his tongue over his lips, and moved
a step back. "No, it ain't nothin' like that. I just knew her on the
streets, that's all."

A whisper of icy air brushed my back, arms, face. "If you were
her pimp, don't tell me. I'd rather not know."

He shrugged, noticed the officer waiting to clear the floor,
sashayed out. At the doorway he turned. "I'm just takin' a time

out from the streets, you see what I'm sayin'? A little R&R. My homies, they be keepin' things cool for me."

I called after him, "When you get back use some of the information you've been given here to help a child. Start with just one. You'll be amazed at how you feel."

After the officer cleared the floor, he stopped by my office. "You can't save 'em all, Jan."

"I'm not trying to save them! I'm trying to give them some thinking tools so they can start saving themselves." I could get so indignant, so impatient with officers who seemed to think I was wasting my breath.

The officer laughed. "You're so serious. Well, that's okay. I figure it this way. Even some of the smart-ass punks are going to remember something you said, whether it was in class or what you shouted down the hall to them to get them thinking. Right now they've got nothing but time to think."

True enough, and more of them thought about reparenting than I hoped. Some of the most resistant and rebellious PSR students enrolled in my classes or came to open door sessions to make something for a child, or for Mom. The simple things they made in parenting lab were similar to art projects children do through grade school and helped them grow up too. Others stopped by my classroom or office, said they were just hangin', then asked a question that opened a door enough for me to give them more information and steer them toward learning lab or Adult Basic Education teachers who knew how to teach them at their level of learning.

That, too, was a choice to reparent themselves. They sent themselves to school.

One PSR week began with a young black man who refused to respond when I called roll. "I's a miss-oh-guy-ness, I don't be answerin' to no woman," he said.

"Missile guy?" someone said, which gave me the extra second I needed.

"Misogynist?" I wrote the word on the board and suggested he learn to pronounce it if he intended to hide behind it. He, too, became one of my followers, though he remained an annoyance through PSR week. As we wrapped up on Friday morning, another man, an old con, waited to tell me he admired me for the work I did. "I have to hand it to you," he said, "the stuff you tell these guys, the way you handle them. You've got balls."

He meant it as a compliment. I thanked him and watched him go, thinking, *Balls, said the queen—if I had them I'd be king.* I'd like to acknowledge the quote's source, but can't find it in my Bartlett's.

17 It's About Time

The officer who said I was so serious was right, and maybe the old con who said I had balls was too. I grew up with a strong work ethic at my core and wore it like a mantle. My parents worked hard, without complaint, and I tried to do the same. I pushed inmates to find worth at the center of their beings, to lift themselves from prison malaise and personal moral decline to make time work for them.

Time is what inmates do. They can be overheard saying, even singing, "If you can't do the time, don't do the crime." As Dewayne, a black man who spoke from experience, said, "Real time stops when you enter prison, and doing time begins." He represented inmates in the Project Social Responsibility planning stage and remained an activist for black inmates' rights through his incarceration.

Dewayne was an articulate man who referred to other black men as brothers and knew black history well enough to teach it. He understood sentencing practices too, and though he never worked as my TA, he mentored me in the sense that he let me see what I read in the law through an inmate's eyes. He spent untold hours in the prison law library and became a walking, talking resource. Now and then, when he could break away from his law clerk job, he spoke to a PSR group about doing time.

"You've got to fit time into the frame," he said. "First, you need to know how much time you're sentenced to do, and how much you can get off for good behavior. Earned time, the system calls it. If you have a long sentence, you need to get into the law library to start working on an appeal. Even if an appeal isn't going to happen, you want to get a look at the law, make sure your time fits your crime."

Men nodded as he spoke, and I made notes so I could better help another man, another classroom full of men. I'd heard it before, from my female students, from the beginning, but hearing it isn't living it.

"How many you here, especially you brothers, met your public defender five minutes before you went into court?" Dewayne asked. Hands shot up. "How many you agreed with whatever he said?" The same hands waved.

"Hell," Dewayne said, looking at me, "at least half these guys don't even know what crime they copped to."

He spoke from experience: He'd been eager to get out of an overcrowded county jail cell, where he slept on a mat on the floor, breathed in bad breath and body odors, and listened to men cry out in their sleep. Prison, he'd heard, was a walk in the park compared to county jail.

"When my public defender ran it down for me, the case the prosecutor had against me and what I could plea to, I said, 'Bring it on, man, let's just get it over with.' I knew the bus ride was coming. At that point I figured the sooner I got started, the sooner I'd get done. Reality set in sometime later, when I got to the island and saw the old cell house. Maybe I should have done the jury thing."

Most men and women in prison have given up their right to a jury trial, accepted plea bargains, and settled in to do their time. They're advised, and know in a secret corner of their minds, that truths they want to keep buried tend to come out in jury trials, which may result in a much longer sentence. But once inside, they start to wonder if an expensive criminal lawyer could have done better, if a jury would have been sympathetic to their plight. I believe most plea bargains are indeed bargains for the offender, which is why the court uses them. It speeds up the process, imposes less time on the offender than a jury trial might, and clears the docket.

One young Tacoma man learned the hard way. He was given an eleven-year sentence in a plea deal, far too much time, he thought, for what he'd done. He withdrew his original guilty plea and opted for a trial. The family had some prominence and enough money to pay a good attorney.

The jury handed down a one-hundred-year prison term.

Under the plea he could have earned one-third off the eleven years, done a little over seven years, and been out of prison before his thirtieth birthday.

Dewayne believes accepting the plea bargain was a wise choice, given his crime. We distributed copies of the state criminal code's sentencing grid and seriousness levels. He tapped a spot on the grid, told the men to find it. Some needed help: it's an overwhelming document. My TA and I circled the room, made certain all were with Dewayne.

"Here's where the judge sentenced me. Seriousness level ten, X on the grid, offender score two, which means I'd had two prior convictions. You see, time increases for every conviction. Legislature's tightening up on us. My sentence range is sixty-two to eighty-two months. I got seventy-two months, right in the middle. Six years to those of you don't know how to break it down.

"Now, if I look at the crimes in seriousness level ten, nothing fits what I did. My public defender got creative, made my assault beef into a kidnap because I dragged the guy out of the bar before I beat the shit out of him. My original charge is up here at twelve, XII on the grid: assault one. With my offender score, I could be doing as much as 147 months. Go figure."

In his telling, now several years after the event, Dewayne's was a crime of passion. Some dude was messing with his woman, and

Dewayne went looking for him, found him in a nightclub, dragged him out of the crowd to a parking lot, assaulted and seriously injured him.

"*Your* woman," I said. "Do you still see women as property of men?"

Some men hooted, made comments of approval. Of course women were their property. Others watched me with wary eyes. Dewayne rocked his hand. "Not so much so. I'm doing seventy-two months over that . . . woman [I gave him points for not saying bitch], and she's way out of the picture. Waaaayyy out."

Men nodded or slumped lower in the old chair desks; some muttered pejoratives and looked away from my raised left eyebrow.

Inmates talk time all the time. "How much time you get?" "I don't have much time." "Me, I gotta lotta time to do." "I lost some 'good [earned] time.'" "I'm trying to get credit for jail time served." (Weeks or months served in county jail prior to a trial or hearing are credited against the sentenced time.)

When inmates talk time, they generally use months. Thirteen months, twenty-one months, sixty-eight months. "It's a give-away," TA Rafael Gomez told them. "You get out, you meet a chick you want to impress, she asks how long you've lived in the area or been at a job, thirteen months pops out before you think. If she's a little streetwise, she says, 'Where'd you do your time?' You could add that to the program. Teach the guys to say, 'Little over a year, almost two years,' forget the months even in here. Answer like civilians."

Even after working in prisons for eighteen years, after listening to countless men and women describe their lives inside, I do not understand the reality of doing time, of being confined to a prison cell, of always looking out through chain-link fences topped with razor wire. For some young men, it's almost a rite of passage.

Young black males who came through Project Social Responsibility said, "You be black in this here society, you be goin' down." (Bureau of Justice statistics indicate 10 percent of black males age twenty-five to twenty-nine are in prison.) They said it with anger edged with pride. They fit a norm, albeit a negative one. I asked them how it made them feel and challenged them to write essays about their perception that young black men get fingered first, almost without a police investigation taking place. "Write about your feelings, your mothers' worries and warnings." Now and then one did. It made thought-provoking reading.

Unfortunately, many I urged to write couldn't; they literally could not write because they couldn't spell words or construct sentences or even verbally define a paragraph. They were illiterate. At any given time, a large percentage of the prison population nationwide reads below fourth-grade level. These are not just inner-city blacks, not just men and women for whom English is a second language, many of whom are illiterate in their native tongue.

As I saw more and more seemingly illiterate young men come through PSR, I began asking if they understood their prison sentences. What part of the criminal justice system made sense to them? They'd been arrested, booked, taken to arraignment, where the charges against them were read aloud. If they were lucky, someone might tell them the time connected with the charges. They had the right to have their presentence investigation report read too, if they couldn't read it themselves, but most didn't. They pretended they could read and signed on the line provided just above their typed name. They were streetwise men, able to recognize their names in print and to sign in cursive of a sort, usually a joined printing. They got by.

How often did I hear "I didn't do nothin', I was just hangin' with my homies when some shit went down" before I figured it out? Many of those young inner-city males were sentenced for anticipatory offenses. Most of them had rap sheets; they weren't innocent bystanders hauled off the streets without cause, but in some cases they were in the wrong place at the wrong time. A corrections officer on the education floor referred to them as street rats.

"City cops made another sweep, dumped the residue in the prison dumpster."

For my part, I tried to help them understand what happened

when they were "just hangin' with their homies." We read together the explanatory paragraph for anticipatory offenses in the
sentencing grid of the criminal code.

> For persons convicted of the anticipatory offenses of crim-
> inal attempt, solicitation, or conspiracy under chapter
> 9A.28 RCW, the presumptive sentence is determined by
> locating the sentencing grid sentence range defined by the
> appropriate offender score and the seriousness level of the
> completed crime, and multiplying by 75 percent.

Some said, "Huh?" At least they were honest about not understanding. Most said, "Shit," which meant the same thing. If they
were interested, I'd show them the sentencing grid, the number
of months for a given crime—one they asked about with all the
innocence they could muster—and do the math on the board.
Math! Who can do math? They could do street deals in their
heads, but not math with pencil and paper. I once considered
math anxiety a female disorder. Not so: most of those streetwise
men drew back when I started multiplying by 75 percent. In most
cases, I referred them to their primary counselors for specific information about their sentences. In all cases, I urged (and sometimes
ordered) them to register for basic education classes. Those patient ABE teachers and their TAs helped those men increase their
skills, which I suspect many put to good use back on the streets.

Primary counselors picked up where public defenders left off,
explaining to inmates how they got the time they were doing, but
counselors are not trained in the law, or Adult Basic Education
skills, for that matter. Try explaining the criminal code paragraph
I quoted earlier, or any other legally worded document, to those
whose comprehension level tests below fourth grade, and who sur-
round themselves with walls higher than prison fences and barbs
sharper than concertina wire.

Over the years, even after Project Social Responsibility was
modified and renamed, and I was free of most of its responsibilities, I maintained my reputation as a safe person to ask tough

questions about almost anything. Men came to me with all man-ner of questions, many of them legal. If we couldn't sort out the answer with the help of my copies of legislative or administrative codes, I sent them to the prison law library to ask an inmate clerk.

I've heard all the snide comments about jailhouse lawyers who spend their time and our tax dollars looking for loopholes in the law, and I've read news stories about frivolous lawsuits coming out of prisons to clog court dockets, but I appreciated those law library clerks. They understood case law, the criminal code, and prison regulations; and they helped me help students. Awareness and un-derstanding, I believe, help all of us cope better with the conse-quences of our behavior.

Now and then I heard on the inmate wireless that jailhouse lawyers, just like those in the free world, weren't cheap. Prison is a moneyless society, but services come with a price—a jar of instant coffee, a couple packs of tobacco and cigarette papers, candy bars, sodas, other things sold at inmate store. A man once asked me if he could have the purple pen I used to grade papers. (I never used red ink for grading: it carried a negative connotation inside the fence.) He said someone in the law library would help him with his case in trade for my purple pen. He threw a little tantrum when I suggested he just buy a pen at store and pay with it. Pens at store had only blue or black ink. Other colors were considered contraband and could lead to an infraction.

I learned early on in my prison teaching career, long before transferring to MICC, to keep pens and pencils in my possession at all times. Set one down anywhere and it was gone. I wore mine over my right ear. For years my white hair had a little purple patch where the pen point poked through it dozens of times a day. Its visibility taunted inmates, one officer told me. I should keep it in my pocket. I said the remark sounded sexist; all pockets are not created equal. He left the issue alone after that. It was a victory of sorts.

I went to the law library clerk who'd allegedly asked for my purple pen to see if the tantrum-throwing student could get the help he needed in some other way.

"You're not giving up your pen, am I right?" the clerk said. I shook my head. He shrugged. "It was worth a try, but here's the straight take on the bro'. It's a waste of time and paper for him to appeal. He'd better stick with school . . . maybe a vocational program . . . otherwise he'll be rippin' and runnin' and doin' life on the installment plan. Even at the low end of thirty thousand per year you taxpayers spend on each inmate, I'd bet he's going to cost you over half a million bucks. You can take that to the bank."

While working on this chapter, I heard a TV news reporter say a man just arrested could get up to fifty-eight years in prison for his crimes. Who calculated his time? She must have determined the time he could receive for each separate crime, but that would also give him three strikes, which automatically means life without parole. Why did the reporter emphasize the time? "Fifty-eight years," she said, as though it were written in bold and underlined. Why do we, the part of society not doing time, find the duration of a sentence so important? What is it we hope doing time will do?

Much is made of time in poetry and prose. Time is teacher, healer, comforter, counselor, friend, and bridge. I believe doing time can teach and heal, and build a bridge back to a meaningful and productive life for those who use their time effectively: those who register for education and work before orientation week ends, take advantage of every program offered, tutor and mentor other inmates.

But after two or three years, they've taken every class they're permitted by state law and grown weary of trying to help those who don't want to help themselves. They're on a waiting list for a correctional industries job so they can pay victim restitution, if they have that obligation, or send money home to support their children. If their earnings are high enough, they pay for room and board in prison, but few make enough. Most will remain on industries waiting lists. Those ordered to pay debts to victims, or to repay debts accrued before they entered prison, generally leave with those debts increased by high interest rates, or they get stuck doing more time with no pay, at taxpayer expense. Does that make sense?

When does doing time stop working for the good of the incarcerated, and therefore for society, and become a negative return? How much time does a felon need to spend in prison to be properly punished? How many more prisons will we need to build, how many more tax dollars will we spend, before we learn to look at the inmate arc—the climb to a personal peak of learning, growth, and behavioral change and the descent to a point where much learned and garnered is lost to time?

Prison is about time. How many years, days, and minutes make time served enough?

18 Men Doing Time

Though I often wondered about specific events in the lives of my students, especially those close in age to my own sons, I didn't ask. So how did I come to know so much about so many? They told me, some more than I wanted to know. They trusted me, even when they didn't like the messages I delivered to them individually and collectively.

One man who'd become so institutionalized he no longer wanted to leave prison told me I reminded him of his mother. He didn't mean it as a compliment, and he may have enrolled in courses I taught so he could point out errors in my curriculum and beliefs. He started with Behavior Management, the class designed to help inmate parents reparent themselves while learning how to parent their children. But Richard had no children. He just wanted to reparent himself because his mother had done such a poor job. It was her fault he was back in prison, and at McNeil Island rather than Washington State Reformatory, his former prison home where he'd earned status in the Lifer's Club, the institution that paroled him to his mother.

A standard life sentence at the time Richard entered prison was twenty years, with one-third off for good behavior, or thirteen years, four months. Men sentenced to life often came together in prison clubs or groups to make sense of doing time. They created items in hobby shops to give as gifts to other inmates' children and often helped new inmates adjust to the reality of prison. Richard did well in such a structured environment.

"See, at the reformatory I've got my time down and nobody hassles me. I do my thing with other lifers, and I get respect because I've got time in. Then I go home, and my mother expects me to get a job before I even figure out the bus route. She's all the time on my case. She figures she's working to provide the home and the food, she's been sending me money through the years, and she wants me to take a job. Any job. Finally, I couldn't stand the nagging so I went out and did a job. Robbed a bank, work I knew how to do."

Richard's classmates watched for my reaction; they saw my left eyebrow climb, and climb more, before I spoke. What words did I choose? I don't recall, but I know they centered on the comfort of blaming others for poor choices, and I know I wrote, "Blaming others keeps you a victim," in huge letters on the dusty chalkboard. I may have added exclamation points, though I tend to avoid such punctuation. Like his mother, and not incidentally the parole board, I would expect him to get a job on release and found his excuse about bus routes weak. I may have opened my mouth and poked in my forefinger, as if his story made me want to throw up, sophomoric theater, I admit.

Then I asked his mother's age (she was in her sixties), set aside silly antics, and got to work. It took most of the quarter for Richard to realize his mother, a divorced woman who'd had all the responsibilities of rearing two sons, was tired. She'd struggled with the reality of Richard's earlier crime, visited him in prison, sent him money, and permitted him to parole to her. She'd lived alone for a very long time and then suddenly had a grown man in her home, one who wanted to take time adjusting to the real world and have good home-cooked meals and an allowance, so to speak, so he could buy a few things he needed. When Richard realized he had pulled his mother back into a developmental stage she had completed twenty or more years earlier because he returned to his own interrupted adolescence, he began to understand. In our last conversation, before he managed a transfer back to the reformatory, Richard said he hoped his mother lived long enough to see him released before she died.

I still think about him and wonder if she has the same hope, or if she fears it will be a rerun of the bad times she's known with him. She's been doing time too.

The message—blaming others for your choices keeps you a victim—blossomed on blackboards, acetate boards, small posters, assignments, and activity sheets for the remainder of my tenure. Parent blame seemed more prevalent among incarcerated men than women, though some of what I term parent blame was levied against government, society, and the system. In the eyes of the blamer, they were all the same; their complaints were adolescent railing against authority. To my knowledge, no scientific study supports my premise that female felons more readily accept responsibility than male felons, but the theory fits my understanding of sex differences and maturation rates.

Brad was another man who took parenting classes even though he wasn't a father. He soaked up information; wrote essays as he learned; and helped students who struggled with spelling, grammar, and sentence structure. One night, when class ended, he dropped a note on my desk with three words in big letters: No Self Esteem.

We'd just completed a unit on building self-esteem in children through encouragement and proper discipline, during which he had grown increasingly quiet. In his self-evaluation at the end of the quarter, Brad wrote an essay about a boy whose mother was a drug addict and prostitute. To me it was an ugly story of a boy who often went out into the night streets to wander while his mother worked; to Brad it was a revelation. He had needed time in prison to separate himself from his mother, and to find a sense of self-worth. He learned far more than positive parenting concepts: he learned he had an inquiring mind, could do well in academic and vocational subjects, could help those with less-developed skills, and had a right to grow up as an individual without the stigma he'd accepted. He served his relatively short sentence and "made it" in the real world.

I often think of those two men as opposite ends of the men-doing-time continuum. Richard blamed a mother who had likely fulfilled her role (at least well enough) for his long-term incarceration, yet he seemed to like his life inside. Brad chose to grow beyond the unpleasant life he had endured with his mother and to establish himself as a responsible citizen. In between were hundreds of men who felt guilt and shame for the hurt they caused their mothers and other family members, and some who continued to blame society's rules for their incarceration. Most found ways to do their time and grew up a little whether they set out to do so or not.

For several months Lonnie, an African American man who had done much of his sentence in an intensive-management unit at another prison, came to the alcove outside my office every morning during one of the ten-minute period movements. I often joined him and asked how he was doing. He always answered, "Same ol', same ol'." He was enrolled in basic skills in a learning lab, where he read at about fourth or fifth grade level and learned early math. He came to talk to me about his family, or his perception of them. Though he never said an unkind word about a family member, he did say, "Life hurts." He had been locked up since about age nine and had liked intensive management, where he was alone, better than MICC, where he was housed in a cell with nine other men.

When a psychological update suggested he needed to return to intensive management, he came to tell me good-bye and thanked me for teaching him about families and parenting on his own. He said it was the most he'd ever talked to a woman. I hadn't realized he saw our ten-minute sessions as a class and include his story as a reminder: we don't always know when we're teaching.

Curt, another black man, dropped by my office regularly to check out my outfit of the day. I sewed most of my clothes in those days (tailored wool or linen suits and dresses, silk or fine cotton blouses), and we discussed padding stitches on the underside of lapels and collars to give them a proper roll, easing in sleeves, quality linings. He knew fabrics, fashion, and how to create a wardrobe that stayed in style. He was a massive man who worked out with weights to stay in shape and kept his head shaved for effect. As he said, no one messed with him. He'd been a tailor's apprentice, sold drugs on the side, gotten caught. He wanted to go back to tailoring and suspected he would give up some of the buffing-up when he got out. Suits don't fit well over such massive chests and biceps, and he wanted to model some of his own creations. He asked me not to tell anyone about his tailoring career. To other inmates, drug dealing was acceptable, an interest in textiles and design was marginal if it went beyond looking good in your threads, and tailoring was just women's work with a fancy name.

Curt was transferred from McNeil Island to a work camp without fences and concertina wire, a step up, a step closer to release. He was eager to go, even if it meant working for the Department of Natural Resources (DNR) planting or thinning trees. Not all men wanted to transfer to work camps, especially camps in remote forested areas. Curt went, determined to go through the process even though he'd never lived outside an inner-city area. His attitude and willingness to do what it took to get beyond prison made him more likely to stay out once released.

Most men I worked with knew when a transfer was pending. All inmates had regular six-month or annual reviews with a counselor or case manager. When time to move on neared, they watched the Daily Transfer Sheet and let their anxiety interfere with school or work performance. Now and then men received an education or job hold so they could remain at an institution, but as the prison population increased, holds decreased. The system moved numbers and crime classifications, not men. Empty beds filled with men who had earned enough points for less restrictive settings, men who had lost points and were being disciplined, and men a staff member wanted moved. Male inmates are always on the move. Many overcrowded jail and prison systems refer to some inmates as "on the bus," on the move until a bed opens.

The Daily Transfer Sheet, distributed to all areas of the institution, included a list of men leaving MICC and their destinations, a list of men moved to or from AdSeg (the Hole), cell and living-unit changes, job assignments and changes, and lay-ins and call-outs. Lay-ins are used for illness and cell confinement, call-outs for movement to an area not generally open to an inmate. I started holding open-door sessions at MICC to avoid the whole process of call-outs for men who needed assistance with Office of Support Enforcement paperwork, or with letters to court or other agencies about their children.

One man who heard I wrote "good letters" asked for help with correspondence with a superior court judge in a rural county. Paul wanted to explain his plans to care for his son, who was living with an older female relative. A dependency hearing regarding the child's placement loomed. Paul feared the state would soon file for termination of his parental rights because of his incarceration and the disappearance of the boy's mother. The current caregiver, Paul's aunt, was in poor health.

Paul arrived at MICC mid-quarter, registered for a parenting class, caught up, and read text materials for other parenting and family courses not being taught that quarter. I helped him with his correspondence, then wrote a letter to the court stating what course-work he had completed. I'd written similar letters for women for years, and I found the men wanted and needed them too. Paul was the first man I taught who filed to gain primary custody of a child whose mother was out of the picture.

Though state law requires that parents only be represented, not present, at dependency hearings, someone at MICC thought Paul and his son deserved a chance. He was escorted to his county's court, where he stated his case. He received custody of his son, and to his surprise a ten-day early release from prison. Ten days may not sound like much, but it means a superior court judge and the Department of Corrections saw worth in him as a person and as a father. He had completed a treatment program for his drug-related crime, and he said he'd learned his lesson. He'd nearly lost his child.

Word got around that Paul got custody and ten-day early release. There was some general grousing that he wouldn't have gotten either were he black and from Seattle, but a black Seattle man disproved that toward the end of my MICC days.

During the first few years I taught at MICC, I taught one or two classes a week at the Annex, an honor camp about three miles from the main institution. Most of the men there did hard physical work during the day and took classes at night for specific skill development. I liked working with them and always enjoyed the short drive outside the fence, even though the Pierce College car was so decrepit its headlights sometimes quit mid-journey. Men at the Annex had more freedom of movement than those inside. There were no fences, just general boundaries.

At one time, well over half of the Annex residents were young Hispanic men with short sentences for drug-related offenses. Most would be transported to Mexico when they completed their time. They did their assigned work, studied English, and congregated in groups with other young Hispanic men for camaraderie and for safety. Most were slight of build, easy marks for prison predators. Rumors of ugly incidents occurring at the Annex abounded, but investigators couldn't get anyone to talk. There are strong bonds among men doing time. Even those not involved in incidents generally won't "snitch out" those who are. When the Hispanic men decided to settle the score, they used a stick (some reports said a baseball bat) to beat an abusive man to death.

Official DOC word said the fight broke out over use of a kiln in the Annex hobby shop. Word on the prison wireless differed: a score had been settled. The version didn't matter. Within hours, all the Hispanic men at the Annex had been transferred from the island to other institutions, and much of the remaining population moved inside the main institution to AdSeg. One of my coworkers who taught English as a Second Language lost her entire class. I lost half of mine. A shroud of silence draped the island. Inmates inside and at the Annex simply didn't talk about it, at least not where they could be overheard.

The public never seemed surprised when such prison incidents made the news. People on the outside rarely heard or read stories of inmates' successes. They certainly didn't know how many incarcerated men earned academic or vocational diplomas, moved up the employment ladder, made amends with their families, started paying child support or restitution, or sent most of their earnings to mothers who had supported them through their bad times.

Though some officers said men flocked to Education because women were accessible there, inmates said they came to learn. School made life inside seem a bit more normal.

We called one short-lived but rewarding attempt to create a more normal environment FACT: Fathers and Children Together. The program gave men enrolled in positive parenting classes an opportunity to interact with their children in a child-oriented space away from regular visiting. There had been a similar and successful program at the women's prison.

Alice Payne, associate superintendent at that time, worked with MICC administrators to find funds for equipment and supplies, hired a professional early-childhood educator to work with the fathers and children, and cajoled the chaplain and staff to provide space in the prison chapel meeting room. While qualified fathers and children met for a few hours in what became a children's center, I met across the hall with mothers and caregivers to present the same basic positive parenting materials the fathers used in my classes.

From the beginning it was difficult to get children transported for the weekday program, which took place while caregivers worked and older children were in school. In evaluating the pilot, we recognized it needed to be offered on weekends in conjunction with regular visiting, but in a separate space. There are many successful programs in place in prisons nationwide, including one now at MICC, where Alice Payne returned as superintendent in the late nineties.

In an odd way, a man I'll call Jerome embodied the determination I saw in many prison fathers to right wrongs done to their children. He struggled to learn positive parenting concepts which differed drastically from the approach his parents had taken. Jerome was on the tall side of average, with ebony skin and searching black eyes. He worked full-time in the prison kitchen and took parenting classes at night. He spoke about his daughter and son with love and devotion, and remorse for their circumstances. They were in foster care and part of a special social services program to give them a better chance in life. Their mother had abandoned them; Jerome didn't think she'd return.

Prior to our first FACT session, Jerome often showed up on the education floor dressed in kitchen whites, a white gauze hairnet over his thick hair and the rubber boots he wore in the kitchen scullery on his feet. He asked questions about specific situations and told me his son, by age four, had learned to ask for a search warrant when police came to the door.

"How do you feel about that now, Jerome?" I asked.

He lowered his head. "Ma'am, it was an awful thing to do. I love those children, and I want them to have a chance, so I'm doing all I can to earn their respect."

On the day of our first FACT meeting, I waited with the group teacher and students, including Jerome, for the caregivers and children to be escorted into the prison and brought to the chapel. The men were nervous. They paced, looked at the clock, looked in a mirror, smoothed their hair. CO's radios crackled, and officers exchanged information. Finally word came that the group was headed our way. The men moved to the chapel steps. I waited inside, watching through the window.

Some children skipped along the sidewalk, uphill from the dock; others clutched women's hands. All were dressed in what looked like their Sunday best, though we had sent word they would be working with paint and other craft materials. There were no black children among them. I stretched for a better look. My chest hurt where my heart must have stopped beating. Had the dock officer who had done the first check-in made a mistake when he called over the official visitor information? Why was Jerome sent to the chapel if his children hadn't made the trip?

I moved outside, ready to console Jerome. Children and caregivers climbed the steps. Jerome stood there grinning, arms open, tears in his eyes, as a boy and girl about eight and ten ran to him and clambered into his arms. He was the first of the group to make introductions.

"Ms. Walker, ma'am, I'd like you to meet my daughter and son."

The other men introduced their children; the escorting officer and chapel CO herded caregivers into our separate room. Delighted children's voices floated on a breeze. Beyond the chain-link and concertina wire fence, sunlight sparkled on the waters of Puget Sound and the MICC ferry returning to Steilacoom. I followed the caregivers into the room where I'd set up tables, an easel, and stacks of materials. The caseworker who brought Jerome's children was unaware of my surprise, and I didn't mention it. I assumed he was their stepdad, a situation that is common in prison, though I knew even then to beware of assumptions.

When the program ended, an officer escorted caregivers and children to the boat, and Jerome went back to work. The FACT teacher and I cleaned up the rooms and locked away supplies: paints, colored paper, children's scissors, glitter and glue, books, and assorted items you might see in a preschool. She ran for a boat; I returned to the education floor and my next responsibility. I didn't see Jerome until the next day, when he poked his head into my classroom just as men were leaving for period movement. He smiled at me, looked down at his wet rubber boots, back at me with tears in his eyes, back at his feet.

"Ma'am, could we talk?"

"Of course, Jerome. Tell me about your children. Did they enjoy the program?"

He nodded, shifted his feet. "I'm sorry for the surprise, ma'am. It's not something I wanted to bring up in class."

Something in his demeanor told me I was wrong about his being stepdad to those two children. "I could see they love you."

"Yes, ma'am."

"Are they adopted?" That would have been quite unusual.

Black children get adopted into white families, but almost never the opposite.

"No, ma'am, they're my children, born to my wife and me during our marriage."

I'm neither doctor nor scientist, but I knew those children weren't his by blood. I closed the door, got him to sit down, and sat beside him. "Jerome, you don't need to tell me anything. I know all I need to know. You love them, they love you, and a caseworker thinks enough of you to keep you and the children together while you do your time."

"Ma'am . . . Ms. Walker . . . I do want to tell you. See, those two were born to my wife during our marriage, like I said. When they were born, I waited for their skin to take on some color, and for their faces to tell me they were mine. Well, the first didn't come to pass. They stayed white. But those faces told me they were mine all the same. If my wife found her pleasures in some other man's bed . . . well, that's life. Those children are mine, right enough, and I supported them all the time I was out there, and I send them money off my books every month."

Jerome was blinking back tears, and I was too. I grabbed the role of toilet paper I kept handy for such times, tore off a length for myself, and left it close enough for him to use if he chose.

He blew his nose. "I love them more than my life. Love them enough to do this time and go on out of here back to the real world and wash dishes for a living this time if need be. Whoever put those children in my wife's body must have done it for me. Seems I can't do it for myself, somehow. The social worker's okay with that, long as I do right by them. Those agencies never got no word out of my wife, and now she's gone they're not like to hear from her."

We both tore off more squares of toilet paper, and I told Jerome I felt privileged to know him and to have met his children. And then I broke a major prison rule, and a legislated one for that matter: I put my hand on Jerome's and gave it a squeeze.

Every man I met at MICC had a story to tell about life's influences and about personal choices. Most of them, like Jerome, will do their time and return to our communities. I saw them as men, students, sons, brothers, husbands, and fathers. They are men doing time, and then they are men who have done time, and finally they are men.

19 Male Inmates as Authors

I gave men opportunities to tell their stories, share their thoughts, and express their feelings in classroom discussions and in daily written assignments I called Writing to Clarify Thinking. Inmates enrolled in college-credit courses completed term papers in addition to writing daily. I'd also emphasized writing with women students, some of whom struggled for a time to find an opening, then wrote vignettes or volumes about their lives. Men deserved an equal opportunity to look inside themselves.

"Write," I'd say to male students, and see blank stares, frowns. "Write? Write what?"

"Write down what you're feeling right now."

Heads reared back. Chairs scraped. "Feelings?"

I'd walk around the room; look at blank papers, squiggles, and doodles; and use the quote attributed to the sportswriter Red Smith, "Writing is easy . . . just open a vein."

Early in my McNeil Island days, an education director decided to take advantage of my determination to get men to write and assigned me a preparatory-level English course. We called it Writer's Workshop; men who considered themselves writers and chose to enroll called it Creative Writing; men assigned the course by the education counselor called it Hell.

Some men who chose the course saw themselves as authors waiting to be discovered; others used writing to fill time and sort life, and thought they might have something to say. Whether skilled enough to be published or mediocre at best, all benefited by working to learn the craft of writing, for somewhere along the learning curve they made self-discoveries that taught them more than most curriculum ever could. One good writer who was reluctant to submit his work wrote in the Farewell Book students created for me, "I'm grateful for . . . your writing class. For me, it was so much more than merely putting words down on paper. I put part of *me* down on paper, and there were those who listened."

Self-awareness. There, in a thimble, was what I hoped to accomplish with all the Writing to Clarify Thinking and Writer's Workshop assignments I cajoled, charmed, and threatened students into writing.

Most of the correctional officers I knew, including Lieutenant Burton, scoffed at my belief in inmates' ability to grow through self-awareness, but I hold the belief as truth and offer it as such.

Eddie, a career criminal who robbed banks with some degree of success, committed burglaries when opportunity permitted, and managed two innovative prison escapes, asked me to critique his life story, written as fiction. He was in his late fifties or early sixties, had some talent and prior training, and had had a few poems published by small (he said obscure) presses. I made several written comments on his work, but I saved what I saw as the most important character revelation for when we talked. As a boy, Eddie had gone into a church during a wedding, stolen from the bride's purse, which she'd left in the dressing room, and then cut a chunk out of the wedding cake that waited in the church basement, and gone on his way.

"Tell me about the nine-year-old boy cutting into a wedding cake and taking off with a piece," I said. He frowned for a moment, then shrugged as if to suggest it wasn't a big deal. I don't think he saw it as very important, certainly not as clever as some of his heists or his escape from a southern state prison. He talked without telling me what I wanted to know, so I told him theories about young boys who steal, which suggest that, regardless of object, the boy is trying to steal love.

"Nah," Eddie said, though he did agree with me about the symbolism of stealing from a bride on her wedding day, and specifically of stealing a piece of wedding cake topped with a bride and groom, thereby ruining the centerpiece of the new couple's reception. He listened to me and read literature about children who steal. He admitted that no other explanation of stealing seemed to fit. There was no peer pressure involved, no test of skill, and no real rush from the deed; he had clearly known it was wrong, and he even felt a little ashamed afterward.

"Why, then?" I asked.

Several weeks later, Eddie told me I was right: he was trying to steal love.

Does it matter? Absolutely. Eddie helped other inmates deal with their time. He may still help them write because he has some talent. His own increased awareness may help them think about what they're writing. He was a mentor even if he denied the role.

Collin was another talented writer who needed little more than steering away from clichés, participial phrases, and adverbs. He wrote with pathos, though some of his stories were too brutally descriptive for my taste. He'd been born in Northern Ireland and had watched his dad and other relatives die in the streets. He came to the United States in his early teens when his mother remarried and moved here. From all accounts, his criminal behavior, which included weapons theft and then torture of the person he believed had identified him, reflected the horrors of his early childhood and his view that any means serves the end. He was righting wrongs done to his family and all Irish Catholics; he was avenging his dad's death, expunging the six-year-old's memory of seeing guns pointed at the father's head, hearing them fire, and watching the father's head disappear, the father die. I suspect writing saved his sanity, and I would not be surprised to see his work in print one day, though he will likely die in prison. He was moved from McNeil Island to another prison for trying to escape. An inmate he'd trusted "snitched" on him. It wasn't his first experience with being "fingered."

Therein lies the making of a good story. I hope Collin writes it rather than acts on it. Snitches are never safe after they've given up information.

Sam, the man whose farewell note I quoted, wrote poetry that met criteria that literature professors teach, but he hid most of it or sent it out to someone he could trust would keep it locked away for him. He also wrote prose, including an outstanding morality short story. I encouraged him to submit his work. He tried once, without success. Perhaps he will try again and one day share his talent with the world. His personal story unnerved me a bit, but Sam needed to write it, and he needed others to hear it.

Many men wrote heartfelt poetry. I read all they brought me and encouraged them to write more. Many also wrote fictional accounts of their crimes and demeaned law enforcement and correctional officers, prison staff, and almost anyone in a position of authority. I told each writing class that I would not read such writing and they wouldn't receive credit for it. Nor would I read pornographic writing, or anything depicting physical or sexual abuse. Over the years two men asked to drop my writing class because I didn't permit freedom of expression. I signed withdrawal forms for both. One came back later and said he'd grown up, had gotten most of his "dark stuff" out of his system, and would like to work on his skills.

Dan, a man who liked to write editorials about discrepancies in the criminal justice system, also wrote about a motorcycle he had found in an old barn and bought from the farmer for a small percentage of its value, because the man saw something he liked in Dan. The bike had belonged to the farmer's son, a Vietnam War casualty. Dan wrote with passion about the bike and his first ride, his first real taste of freedom after being released from jail. It was a spiritual story, and a story of spirits, for some unseen force saved Dan from death in a blind turn on a steep grade. He pondered the event and his insatiable appetite for drugs. His parents and sister came to an island graduation program. His was a supportive and pleasant family. Why did he seem to need time in prison? I saw in him a gentle man who loved all living things. I hope he keeps writing until he exorcises the demon that keeps him going back to drugs.

Clive used his skills to write the curriculum for a specialty course. Unfortunately, credit for the writing went to the instructor who hired him as a teaching assistant. Clive's own story revealed a man who had had some success as a minor league baseball player, but who didn't know how to act in society, who emulated others, who escaped from his fears with heroin, and who ultimately found his way to prison, where he earned a college degree and perhaps learned a sense of worth.

Men wrote about fathers who abused them with assorted weapons and fists, fathers who abused them in the name of religion, and fathers who set the pattern of criminal behavior and expected their sons to follow suit. Men wrote about children lost to them because the children's mothers disappeared. They wrote about "messing up" at minimum-custody work-release facilities they hated so they could return to the womb of medium-custody prison. One light-skinned black man wrote about racism until he discovered his own racist attitude kept getting him in trouble. Then he wrote about his black father, a man unknown to him, and how he felt about a man who had abandoned a woman and child. He was very bright and had much to offer others with similar experiences, but he responded to encouragement with grunts, and once a little grin. I trust the universe helped him find his way. And one man wrote a story about coveting the bread in a sandwich he saw me eating one registration day. The bread had hazelnuts and whole grains and was quite good. I was grabbing bites midafternoon of a thirteen-hour workday, trying to be discreet, checking registration forms while I ate. Not long before, the men had been to Mainline, where they were served a large meal. They were using my room as a waiting room.

"Did the bread look like it would be worth giving up crime, and drugs, for ever and all eternity?" I asked.

"Could be," Doug said.

I hope it was worth it, just as I hope all the men who authored stories about their sorrows and losses, their regrets and shame, have found their way back to society. As I said to Lieutenant Burton one chain day, every inmate has a story. Writing frees the spirit and reveals the soul, even for those who will never again live outside the fence.

20 Women Doing Time

Studies of sex differences indicate females score higher in verbal skills, males in spatial relationships. A popular book suggests men and women are from different planets. Correctional officers, especially male COs, who have worked with both men and women in prison say men are easier; give them males to guard any day. When pressed for how they differ, or why men are easier, they fall back on clichés, most of them having to do with hormones, most of them unkind to women. I researched the psychology of sex differences rather extensively as part of a graduate-studies program, worked with both female and male offenders, and formed some opinions that developed into beliefs.

Women with whom I worked tended to call their living-unit rooms their "house," as in "I left my homework back in my house." Men at MICC tended to refer to their living-unit rooms as cells long after the old cell house was a memory and they resided in two-men rooms off large, well-lighted dayrooms.

Many women formed and joined family groups inside prison. I considered them families of survival, as important while doing time as their families of origin and families of procreation had been outside the fence. I learned a little about how they functioned, though I didn't probe too deeply, just as I wouldn't ask prying questions about their families in the real world. Some women talked openly; others said little.

"Mom" was usually a mature woman who had successfully reared children and had extensive life experiences not associated with criminal behavior. She described her crime as one of passion or need, carried out to protect or provide for her real-world children. In her real-world life, she often performed both traditional mother and traditional father roles, by necessity, not by choice.

"Dad" was usually a woman younger than Mom, without children of her own, who had committed an aggressive crime she described as "getting her share," or "evening the score." Some women who assumed the father role also declared themselves lesbian, but some did not. Dad's relationship with Mom was usually not sexual.

Their prison-family children were almost always young inmates, many of whom had children of their own but little emotional or financial support from outside the fence. They relied on their prison mom and dad to help them cope with crises inside prison and out. As children will do, prison children acted out when they didn't like their parents' advice. Their prison parents used consequences for such behavior, often ignoring their children to the point of shunning. Children do not like being ignored; those inmate children found ways back into the family circle.

Though I never suggested women enrolled in my classes should consult their prison mom or dad, or talk things over with others in their survival family, I knew they did. They told me about their discussions. In several instances, I had moms and children in the same parenting class. I provided information and stimulus for thinking through decisions, urged those who needed help beyond education to get psychiatric counseling, and photocopied materials for prison dads who dropped by the classroom to ask questions.

My unscientific study, or perhaps I should say observation, fits much of what is known about sex differences. Women's lives tend to center around family.

Many female offenders also formed significant-other relationships while inside, though not all who moved into such pair groups considered themselves homosexual. They maintained their hetero-sexual relationships through phone calls and letters, and occa-sional visits. They engaged in deprivation homosexuality, the often intense homosexual relationships that develop between per-sons in situations such as prison. When they returned to a hetero-sexual society, most also returned to heterosexuality. I taught those concepts as part of interpersonal relationships courses and wrote about them in *My Relationships, My Self*, a book that grew from my frustration with adapting standard family relationships texts to a population that didn't fit most norms.

In short, women did not exhibit the extreme homophobic re-actions I saw with men, which I described earlier. Most women were comfortable with hugging and even kissing in public, some-times for shock value. The prison staff viewed such behavior with varying degrees of acceptance. The same infractions used against incarcerated males applied to females. Engaging in sexual acts with the exception of spouses during extended family visits vio-lated rules and regulations, and those caught were infracted. But keep in mind that many women say they seek the cuddling close-ness of a relationship more than sexual release. The prison librar-ian told me she often disrupted cuddling in the library, a meeting place for women who formed significant relationships but lived in separate housing units.

One woman who came to me with her own particular concern about sexual issues had a complaint about another teacher. I didn't listen to such complaints, but the woman blurted it all out so fast I couldn't stop her. In a British accent, Altheda said, "The typing teacher is depraved. She makes us type the most ghastly sentence over and over: 'The penis mightier than the sword, the penis mightier than the sword.' I shot my husband in his, you know."

She shoved her typed exercise sheet in front of me, and indeed she had typed that line the length of the page. I changed "penis" to "pen is," explained it was a quote, assured her the typing teacher was not supporting male superiority, and listened to spe-cific details of the ghastly husband who had used his penis in a rather swordlike way until she shot him there. Her only regret, at the time she described the shooting, was his survival and recovery from the wound. She realized, after the fact, that a shot through the heart would have served better, but she'd long since decided the man was heartless, so really, what else could she do?

I did not laugh. I handled the situation with the aplomb of a confessor. When I had a break, I made all my students leave the classroom, locked the door, walked down the hall with a stride that said move aside, unlocked the staff-room door, and then the restroom door. Safely locked inside, I turned on both faucets, flushed the toilet, and laughed until tears ran. Then I washed my face and carried on. I didn't tell Altheda's story until several years later, when it seemed to fit a meandering discussion in Project Social Responsibility at McNeil Island. Few men laughed; most stared. A male colleague later said men do not like women to say penis, regardless of what they might like women to do with one.

Many women doing time had used a gun to retaliate against a controlling or abusive man. When they talked about shooting, they said things like "I wouldn't be doing time if I hadn't reloaded the gun, but five shots weren't enough"; "I shouldn't have shot him when he was asleep"; and "Shooting him at work wasn't the smartest." They had been passive women, victims of physical, sexual, and emotional abuse that escalated until they ended it by killing the abuser. Most of those women said they knew at some level it was him or them.

Many researchers say the same thing. What starts with conventional or routine slapping or pushing does lead to more dangerous abuse. If it is not stopped, there's a high likelihood the victim will die.

During my tenure at the women's prison, a decree came down ordering all women convicted of murder to be confined in the maximum-security unit for a percentage of their sentence, and to wear the standard orange coveralls male inmates wore during transport. Until then, female inmates had dressed in civilian clothes they had brought from home, procured from a clothing room filled with donations from the community, or inherited from prior inmates.

The orange coveralls didn't fit women's curves, but rules were rules. At first the women were allowed to wear undershirts and zip the top as far as their figures permitted but someone found an unzipped front provocative, even with a state-issued undershirt to the neck, so a new zipped-front edict came down. Coveralls drooped from women's shoulders like shrouds, sleeves clumped above their wrists, waistbands settled around hips, crotches at knees, and six or eight or ten pant-leg rolls surrounded their ankles.

"This is ridiculous," I said to the male unit supervisor. "I understand the reason for uniforms, but they need to be made for women's bodies."

"Or use another solution," he said. "Line 'em all up and shoot 'em. That's pretty much what they did to their men."

I'd grown accustomed to such comments and ignored his suggestion. Instead, I lined those women all up, so to speak, and taught them a college-level family relationships course. We were locked in the Max dayroom, a narrow room with one barred window to the grounds and one small window to the corridor. Their individual rooms along the same corridor also remained locked at all times. They pushed a button, or more often yelled, when they wanted out. I understood why they resorted to yelling: more than once I waited, and waited, after ringing for an officer to come unlock the dayroom door. Officers in Max control also answered phones, oversaw movement into and out of AdSeg, took restroom breaks, and in some cases didn't give a damn about women who wanted out of a locked room. Those doors, in those years, couldn't be buzzed open; someone had to walk down the hall and insert a key.

The dayroom had a spider table—a large, round metal table with attached stools. As there were more of us than stools, students carried in chairs from their rooms, but that defied regulations. Chairs could be used as weapons or battering rams. If we couldn't all fit around the table, some had to sit on the floor. Suck it up; education is a privilege.

Hall mirrors were allegedly positioned so a control officer could see what transpired within the room at all times. One officer, in an attempt to unnerve me, joked about locking me in with murderers and leaving me there. (He, like the unit supervisor, considered educating female felons a waste of money.) Prior to taking on the group, I'd been briefed on their criminal history. All had committed one crime: murder. None had prior arrests. They came from cities, small towns, farm communities. They were intelligent, interested, and interesting women. I loved teaching them. Unfortunately, my enthusiasm must have been too evident: I was permitted to go into that situation during only one quarter. The male education director said those women had plenty of time to do and would be out in open population sooner or later. They could take my classes then. We viewed time differently: he'd fled Uganda in a bloody uprising and patiently waited for a safe time to return to his roots. Though I understood his reasoning, I disagreed with his decision.

I do not condone murder, but I do understand those women considered it their only recourse. Until they killed to escape violence and abuse, the women in that group had not been violent. To a woman, they felt freer inside the prison fence than they had felt in their own homes, and they used their time to advance their education, improve skills, grow in awareness, nurture their children as best they could from inside, and help other women struggling with similar life patterns. And to a woman they agreed that no one can be helped out of abusive relationships until they're ready to abandon all hope for change; risk the fallout their children experience; and leave behind, perhaps forever, life as they have known it.

Ellen made such a choice. She moved her young children to a relative's home, continued working to support them, and lived in her car, which she parked in a different place every night. The man found her. She emptied a gun into him. Her case didn't go well in court. The arresting officer said there were no signs of struggle, no evidence she'd been assaulted then or ever. It was her word against the evidence—a man dead of multiple gunshots. Witnesses who testified to her fear were discounted. The restraining order she had against him wasn't proof he intended to hurt her the night she shot him. Prior beatings didn't prove he would beat her again. He didn't have a gun. She should have gotten help. She should have gone to a shelter rather than risking her life in a car parked in an underground garage.

Should should should. I heard it too many times. It's an ugly word when used against a victim.

During the years I listened to female felons' stories, I also studied the abuse continuum, talked with professionals who operated shelters and safe havens, and kept hearing "No one can help victims until they're ready to be helped, and for many, that time comes too late." For several years I taught women who ended the abuse continuum by ending their abusers' lives. Later I taught men doing time for domestic violence and pondered anew what makes a man choose to batter the woman he claims to love.

Women convicted of murder made up a very small percentage of those doing time. Most of my students had committed drug or property crimes (robbery, burglary, embezzlement), or both, as drug use often leads to theft. Some of my first students claimed to be riding their "old man's" beef, particularly drug-delivery charges, because women received lighter sentences. That was prior to determinate sentencing laws, at a time when judges used their discretion rather than a sentencing grid and inmates waited for parole board hearings to learn when they'd be released.

Members of the parole board came to the women's prison once a month to review cases of those whose time and crime earned them a hearing. "It's board day" echoed across the compound, and women scheduled to meet the visiting board members came to class dressed to the nines, makeup in place (often overdone), fingernails chewed to the quick. Women came out of hearings whooping or crying; their friends waited to cheer or console. Soon another woman appeared in the same nice suit or dress worn earlier by a friend. "You want to look your best. No way do you want to go in front of the board in ratty old clothes."

For some, looking their best meant sexy. One young blonde woman wore a sheer blouse the color of her hair over a bright turquoise bra. She was granted immediate release, then rearrested for prostitution within hours of being bused to Tacoma. "I was just looking to make a little money," she said. "The cops set me up."

Another woman, Luanne, came back from the board fuming. Women use English slang quite creatively. The very air turned blue. No amount of hushing stopped her diatribe. I'd been teaching there so short a time I didn't know whom she was calling "bitch," until another student explained the board had "bitched" her. She'd been classified a habitual criminal and sentenced to remain in prison indefinitely for accumulated property crimes over several years. (Being named a habitual criminal under indeterminate sentencing guidelines is like earning a third strike under three-strikes laws.) As she spewed invectives, I learned about her crimes: She stole to order. If a client wanted a new TV set, a special garment or shoes, any small appliance, Luanne procured it. Her clients came from all walks of life and, according to her, included parole officers.

When she calmed down, we had an interesting discussion about her level of expertise. I knew little about robbery operations, or about those who choose to commit crimes. After she'd schooled me, I said it sounded like she lacked adequate skills for her chosen profession and asked her if she was ready to quit, to earn a living some other way.

"You don't get it. I've been bitched." More colorful language followed. I felt as though I were wading through a garbage dump, but oddly that it was important to keep trudging.

"You also said you're appealing to Olympia [DOC headquarters] to get it overturned and just want to go home to Alaska to take care of your mom."

"Yeah, what of it?"

She was enrolled in a traditional clothing construction class, had completed textile manufacture and care theory quickly and with outstanding grades, and sewed well enough to show me she had capabilities beyond what she called "ripping and running." She was making a pair of flannel pajamas for her mother and had mastered flat-fell seams, not an easy task. She had determination and skill, and love for her mother. Before she won her appeal and was granted release on condition she leave the state and never return, a clothing manufacturer brought its industry to the women's prison. Luanne was one of their first and best employees. She earned enough money to send home. Though I wasn't fond of having a sweatshop industry in the prison, it did help many women earn enough to support themselves, give them employment when they got out, and provide a work history for their résumé when they job-searched. And it helped with their self-esteem, that immeasurable quality that makes a difference.

Luanne, and the other women who became my first students when the community college took over education responsibilities at the prison, struggled with the change from local school district to community college. They liked the gregarious home economics teacher I replaced, considered the traditional classroom a refuge from prison, and feared change. The community college budget would not support programs as they had known them.

The first time I unlocked the sewing lab cupboards, I stepped back in shock. Shelves held enough fabric, thread, zippers, bias tape and trim, needles, tape measures, thimbles, and other notions to rival the dry-goods section of a neighborhood variety store. Dressmaker patterns filled three large file cabinet drawers.

Word that community college instructors would do a complete inventory swept across the campus. Women flocked to classrooms to help. At least a dozen women told me they'd been the departed teacher's assistant and that she'd promised them fabric and supplies: the blue linen, the flannel with pink roses, packages of bias tape or needles, spools of thread. I listened, laughed sometimes when their lines were especially clever, and learned to unlock one cupboard at a time, even with the classroom door locked. Still, supplies disappeared. One rather large woman whose hands weren't quicker than my eye stuffed the front of a peasant blouse with supplies. When I said, "Untuck your blouse at the waist before you leave the room," she did; looking open-mouthed at the mound at her feet, she said, "How did those get there?"

Experienced staff told me she was certifiable. When the prison added a Special Needs Unit, she was moved there on the basis of psychiatric evaluations. Years later I encountered her in an emergency waiting room where I'd taken a family member. "Jan," she said, "do you remember me? I'm your friend Penny from the women's prison. We were there together."

"Together, but in different capacities," I said, glancing about. It was two in the morning; not many in the waiting room cared, but I added, "I teach at McNeil Island now." When she asked for my address and home phone number, I declined and wished her well.

As my family member and I were leaving, the receptionist told me Penny visited them regularly. "She's a bit odd," the receptionist whispered.

"Yes, I've met her before," I said. She must be doing something right if she's living in the free world and dropping in for late night visits at a hospital emergency room.

Sherry, a dark-haired woman, attractive though exceedingly thin with the sunken cheeks and damaged teeth of a long-term bulimic, told me that she had a sewing machine in her house (living-unit room) that she used to sew for indigent inmates, and that she needed to pick up fabric she'd been promised for those poor, unfortunate women. I said a machine was missing from the classroom inventory and was listed with other missing items on a trace sheet going to all areas of the institution. She brought the machine back within minutes, though it disappeared again off and on during the time she remained in prison. She always had authorization from someone to use it overnight, for the weekend, for the duration of a school break.

Sherry fascinated me. She garnered trust from those she robbed and managed to charm her way out of infractions until she was hired as a clerk for a psychiatrist, stole checks from the woman's handbag, and landed in AdSeg. The only other consequence she suffered over the years she spent in prison was at the hands of an inmate she had conned with promises of garments she would construct. She had pulled similar scams successfully more than once because inmates who paid her were reluctant to snitch and perhaps unable to get even. But Sherry finally met her match: She collected fifty dollars from an older woman, spent it at store on food items that she ate and then purged, and came to me with her tale of woe. The older woman threatened to break her arms and legs if the promised garments didn't appear.

Sherry and I had a long talk about her problems. She sobbed when I refused to give her fabrics she believed were hidden somewhere in the education building. (They weren't.) I urged her to get help, to tell her primary counselor her concern. She left miffed and went to the education director with her plea. The next time I saw Sherry, she had been beaten, though no bones were broken. Her attacker allegedly had procured a large glass juice bottle, wrapped it in a paper bag, and beaten Sherry until glass shards poked through the paper.

Sherry was released from prison soon afterward and was arrested within days in a small Oregon town where she forged checks stolen from a benefactor she'd charmed.

Clothing construction classes lasted for several years as a vocational preparation program and self-esteem builder at the women's prison. Most of the time a teaching assistant ran the sewing lab while I taught the academics of textiles and garment construction and care, or conducted parenting or family lectures in another part of the room. The classroom, a designated security nightmare, opened into a sewing lab with two four-by-eight-foot cork-topped cutting tables in the middle, sewing stations along the far window wall, a curtained dressing room, and a load-bearing divider wall separating the whole from a kitchen/dining room. Cabinets suspended from the ceiling added to the dining room's privacy and made the kitchen dark. The first time I drew keys for the room, the key control officer said, "Good luck with all those hidey-holes," handed me a ring with eighteen keys, and flashed a grin that said I'd need more than luck.

The dining room became our lecture room. I borrowed a portable blackboard from another program and seated women around the dining table. It was common in our classrooms in those years to teach several courses at once, and those who enrolled in clothing construction classes soon enrolled in parenting and family courses too. Even if they didn't, they overheard enough to take some valuable information with them on their release.

Traditional home economics courses played an important role for women during those years, but both they and I most valued the parenting classes and the opportunity to work with or observe children in a preschool setting. The community college inherited a cooperative preschool program for three-, four-, and five-year-old children who came in from the community, through the locked gates, across the compound to the education building, and into a locked area known as Pooh's Corner. Parents of enrolled children assisted on a rotating basis and interacted with inmate students completing the lab part of child development or parenting classes. Community moms taught inmate moms firsthand.

Pooh's Corner was open and sunny, with Winnie the Pooh figures painted on the walls, two child-size bathrooms, and all the play stations necessary to provide a complete learning environment for children. Women enrolled in other education programs often stopped to peer in the corridor window. The presence of children mattered to those women. The preschool opened onto a pleasant and safe playground. Women who worked as teacher's aides said they could forget about prison while they watched children on slides and swings. Though Pooh's Corner got good press for many years, it came under attack in the late eighties as a potentially dangerous, undesirable place for children. I disagreed then and disagree still. Children are highly valued by female inmates, who police their own.

Pooh's Corner went from a cooperative preschool to an inmate mothers' and children's gathering place, occupied only on Saturdays. The traditional home economics classroom was gutted and rebuilt for industry use. For a time I taught lecture classes in what had been Pooh's Corner, where students and I sat on chairs meant for preschoolers and bent to write on low tables.

The Ugandan education director and I clashed over curriculum, the funds parenting classes "took away" (his term) from basic skills courses, and the amount of time I spent in court in termination of parental rights cases. (I always made up my time.) We were on a collision course harmful to me personally and to the program. It was time for me to move on, but once I made the decision he begged me to stay. I spent three quarters teaching at McNeil Island three days a week, the women's prison two. Some days I'd waken unsure where I was going. I decided to leave the women's prison to teach men full-time.

Female felons always occupied a special place in my heart, so I went back to the women's prison to visit before completing this chapter. The current education director, Larry Richardson, a former colleague at MICC, showed me around. The prison houses three times more women than when I left. Many of the old buildings are gone. There is a modern, pleasant education building in minimum custody that includes the day-care facility for women involved in the mother-infant bonding program (see chapter 15). While Mom goes off to work, other minimum-custody inmates, supervised by professionals, care for the children as part of their program commitment. The day-care room and playground could be anywhere in America. It just happens to be inside the fence.

The old Max, where I taught women convicted of murder, stands empty, ready to be razed. A new, state-of-the-art close-custody/administrative segregation/special needs building houses those not permitted in open population. The original single-story brick living units are gone, replaced by one multistory, cement-walled building. The inside or medium-custody education building looks much the same, though Pooh's Corner is now a classroom with adult-size desks.

The atmosphere hasn't changed. Women doing time differ from men doing time in manners difficult to explain, though I believe it comes back to those families of survival, the prison connections that make doing time bearable. The women seem more relaxed, more at peace with themselves and comfortable with others. They say hello and move easily into conversation. I talked with a woman doing life without possibility of parole, the first so sentenced. She had been my student when she first entered prison in the 1980s, then an eighteen-year-old girl. She caught me up on other lifers, some now out and doing well, some still in where they help others. I asked about Mai, a Native American woman who had been one of my earliest students, and learned she's housed in minimum custody, though she had been out at prerelease for a time. It didn't surprise me she hadn't adjusted. She arrived in prison with limited English skills and little sense of culture outside the reservation. She once told me she'd taken pieces of broccoli from the dining room, dried them, and sent them out to her mother with a letter saying, "They make us eat little trees here."

I have a letter she wrote me just before I left the women's prison in 1990. She was housed in Max at the time for one transgression or another and sent the communication out through proper channels. I saved it and quote one line from it: "The struggle of my Indian ways are hard for me, but I must be strong."

Strength is a recurring theme with incarcerated women. On the pleasant spring day I visited, women sat in groups on the lawn outside their living unit, enjoying fresh air until recall. Some sat quite close, as female inmates always have. Touch is the norm for them, not a sexual approach, as it would be in male prisons, but a need. They are mothers, separated from their children and moms, sisters, and aunts. My old nemesis Lieutenant Burton, who transferred to the women's prison a few years back, would remind me they didn't get sent to prison for jaywalking, or some such, but some of them got there because they followed a man onto the criminal path. That is not an excuse, but remains a truth.

Somewhere, their children are doing time too, and so they must be strong.

21 Inmates and Victims Face-to-Face

Inmates meet some of their victims face-to-face when family members visit. Their families, especially their children, are indirect victims of every crime. I saw pain and delight on inmate mothers' faces when their children joined them in prison programs. I heard them whisper, "I've hurt my children, that's the worst."

In one women's prison program, in which caregivers brought children to Pooh's Corner and stayed along with the children's mothers, one inmate mom saw the physical damage the illegal drugs she had taken during pregnancy had inflicted on her child. At nine months, baby Shea couldn't sit or roll over; her spine wouldn't support such normal activities, and the prognosis wasn't good. Shea's caregiver, a woman with a well-padded body, held and rocked her several hours a day. When the inmate mother, a lean, flat-chested woman, took Shea in her arms and sat back in the rocking chair, the baby screamed, and her arms and legs jerked. She didn't stiffen in protest as most nine-month-old babies would. She couldn't, nor could she push with her arms or kick her feet. Her little legs remained crossed scissor-fashion, a telltale sign of drug interference during fetal development.

While the young mother sobbed, the caregiver shook her

head. "It's too late now, isn't it? They don't learn in time, do they? Their babies suffer forever."

In the early 1990s, a group of crime victims and their families came together to make their voices heard, their suffering known. In cooperation with the Department of Corrections, the group began confronting inmates through a program called Victim Awareness. The group fought to gain rights for victims similar to those given by law to criminals. They united on the strength of shared grief and anger, and they grew to become an important component of the DOC's work to make offenders accountable for their crimes.

"Criminals," the victims' group argued, "have the right to an attorney at taxpayer expense if they can't afford their own. They have the right to remain silent when arrested, the right to plead not guilty when charged, the right to a trial by a jury of their peers. What about their victims? What rights did they have?"

Victims, their families and friends, and entire communities were incensed by the ease with which several offenders had walked away from work release during the 1980s to commit abhorrent atrocities, the same atrocities that motivated MICC to design and implement Project Social Responsibility. The victims' group argued the crimes could have been foreseen: the offenders' records, they believed, indicated those men were not good candidates for release. One had threatened revenge against witnesses to his earlier crime and had enacted it, killing two adults and an eight-year-old girl. He was sentenced to death; the sentence has since been carried out, but as the victims' group said, that didn't give people back their loved ones. Members wanted criminals to know how it felt to be victimized; they wanted criminals to stop committing crimes. And they wanted specific information about individual felons.

They campaigned for classified information about their victimizers' treatment and progress during incarceration, and for advance notice when those men or women were transferred from one institution to another, especially from maximum- or medium-custody prisons to minimum-custody camps, pre- or work release, or community corrections/parole status. They wanted permission to attend classification hearings and to have their voices heard by those making the decisions about felons who had victimized them, their families, and their communities.

They also wanted financial compensation for the expenses incurred for physical and psychological injuries. "Consider a crime scene where offender and victim are both injured and need medical attention," the group's leader said. "On arrest, the offender's injuries must be tended at taxpayer expense. Arresting officers are responsible for seeing to the offender's transport to a medical facility. Though officers may also call for transport and attention for the victim, taxpayers do not pick up those costs. The victim does."

Crime victims often say they want those who offended against them or their families to remain incarcerated forever, an understandable but unrealistic wish. About 95 percent of all convicted felons eventually leave prison. Rather than standing helpless in the shadow of justice and sentencing laws, the victims' group started working with DOC and community college personnel to design an education program. The program, which still exists in a modified format, challenges offenders to empathize with crime victims and identifies intervention strategies to reduce chances of reoffending.

I attended a quarter-long Victim Awareness class at Tacoma prerelease and then facilitated one at McNeil Island for two quarters. I admired the victims' group's efforts and the program that members helped bring to prison, but I found the classes beyond the pale. Victims came into the prison classroom with their stories, and with stark video accounts of egregious crimes. The victims who gave their time in the Tacoma area included survivors of child abuse, child sexual abuse, and rape; a sibling and a spouse of a rape victim; parents of murdered children; the mother of a Tacoma boy sexually mutilated by a man who had walked away from work release; the director of a local victims' group; and representatives from the Sexual Assault Crisis Center and Mothers Against Drunk Driving.

One of my colleagues dubbed the class Guilt 101.

Early Victim Awareness classes were indeed heavy on guilt and blame, without what I saw as an adequate balance of opportunity for offenders to change. Facilitating the program was added to (I like to say heaped on) my increasing hours in Project Social Responsibility and parent/family lecture courses. The first students were handpicked by classification staff. I read those students' records, listened to victims tell their stories, watched depressing videos, distributed assignments, collected completed work and read it all, wrote weekly reports, and met with each inmate student to help him keep the information in perspective so he could find ways to use it for his own growth and development. But facilitating a program differs from teaching a class, and in truth I am a teacher. I did not find facilitating rewarding.

In fact, I hated it.

As part of the course objectives, inmate students were asked to identify five feelings they had about their victim(s) and five ways their behaviors affected victim's lives. Unfortunately, those men hadn't been trained to recognize and identify feelings and hadn't given much thought to the aftermath of their acts. They got caught up in intellectualizing the events. They spoke in terms of thoughts, evident in comments such as "I feel that it was wrong of me." When I asked where in their body they felt evidence of the wrong, they said, "Huh?" Getting to remorse takes work. The men selected to participate in the group had not been through Project Social Responsibility, so they lacked awareness of basics we covered there. One man said he felt it was wrong of the victim to try to stop him; it was just a burglary, which turned into homicide because the victim came home and got in the way.

Identifying personal patterns of behavior related to the commission of crimes was another objective of the program. Again, because of a lack of background in human behavior or whole system theory, they struggled with the concept. They were being pushed to cope with too much at once. To their credit, they tried to understand it all: concepts and theories, victims' personal pain and reactions, their own and their families' and friends' despair. One man became very depressed as the sessions went on, and one got more and more angry.

Perhaps Trevor, the angry man, wasn't a good candidate for the program. About midway through the quarter, he jumped to his feet, sending his chair desk sprawling. His feet tangled with the desktop and slowed his progress toward the speaker, a man whose son had been killed by a drunk driver. I can only guess what Trevor intended. He later told me he considered the man a pompous ass, a father who couldn't let go. I knew enough about Trevor's case to understand the old feelings the speaker had hooked, but that did neither of us any good. Of course, the incident had to be reported, written up, and investigated.

Trevor, who was also enrolled in another course I taught, went to the Hole, a place worthy of the title: a subterranean maze of small cells off corridors that could have been dug by an underground animal. Focused security lights created eerie shadows. Electric fans circulated exhaled breath and melancholy. I went there with Trevor's assignments and to monitor a final test. Why couldn't security staff observe him take the test, I asked. It wasn't their job, they replied. Officers posted there weren't nose-wipers. How had I forgotten?

Thanks to Trevor's behavior, Lieutenant Burton ordered a "blue uniform" (correctional officer) to attend the remaining Victim Awareness classes, a disaster for our program's goals. Victims were there to speak to offenders, but their eyes settled too often on the officer. Offenders tempered their questions and responses to fit standards of the convict code. Though I argued, even begged, for the officer's removal, the lieutenant's order stood.

Throughout the quarter, I worried about Chayton, the Victim Awareness student who showed signs of depression. His feeling statements, completed at each session's end, worried and then alarmed me. After one particularly graphic presentation, he wrote comments I decided should be seen by the unit counselor who had assigned him to the program. My decision upset Chayton, who asked why I'd gotten the authorities involved. My concern for his well-being rocked him. I was a teacher, a white woman with an education; he was an American Indian, looked down on by teachers and whites all his life. So he believed. We talked about what led to his perception. In time, we talked about other matters, including Native American brotherhood and how to embrace spiritual beliefs while doing time. The system didn't make it easy, though the DOC did permit volunteer spiritual leaders to meet with the men.

Like most Native American men at MICC, Chayton had a medicine pouch in his cell, stored as required in a shoebox. His was wrapped in a state-issued red bandana with an attached feather, its quill bound with leather and heavy thread. With the influx of Bloods and Crips into prison, the order came down that all red bandanas had to be sent out or destroyed.

I don't know what happened next, though I suspect Chayton had no one to accept his package, and possibly inadequate funds to mail it. In the end, Lieutenant Burton came to my office one afternoon with a brown lunch bag clutched in his hand. He stuffed the bag into my briefcase and told me not to look at it until I was off the island, not to ask him a question, and not to mention it to anyone, ever, on pain of serious repercussions. That was over ten years ago, long enough, I trust. The brown bag contained (contains still) Chayton's medicine bag and totem. I keep them in the brown bag for its symbol of simplicity and have them stored to return one day to Chayton.

What I don't know, the missing middle of the story, is what transpired between Chayton and the lieutenant. Neither ever told me, but whatever did happen affected my relationship with both men. I respected Chayton for the humanity and spirituality I saw in him, and I became friends with Lieutenant Burton.

I was relieved of the task of facilitating Victim Awareness after two quarters. In time, it was taught without bringing victims to the classroom. Many of the victims burned out. They wanted to enlighten and confront inmates, and to further their cause, but it took a horrendous toll. They needed to make peace in other ways and move on.

In 1999 Washington state passed the Offender Accountability Act, which focused resources on offenders most likely to reoffend and cause harm to their victims and communities. The act also strengthened reparation and restitution obligations of sentenced felons, all of whom now contribute to a victims' compensation fund. It is a court-ordered obligation. Offenders contribute from their prison employment earnings or from money sent to them by family or friends. All monies earned by or given to inmates are held by the prison accounting office; an established percentage is deducted by the system at each deposit. Inmates draw on the balance in their funds to buy store and hobby-shop supplies, and to cover other expenses they accrue.

Their role in legal changes governing offenders' contributions to a fund available for victims was a major accomplishment for a group of citizens who rallied support among fear-filled, grieving survivors of violent crimes. Unfortunately, it's more difficult to continue collecting from offenders once they're released. There are currently too many loopholes in the law, but that may change. Victims have rights, too, and dedication to their cause.

22 Parenting from a Distance

Parenting responsibility, like crime debt, does not end at the prison gate. Unless relationships are terminated by law, inmate parents have rights and obligations to their children. Parenting from a distance is an emotional commitment they make to do all they're able for their children without criticizing or attacking the children's primary caregiver.

Throughout my early years in correctional education, I collected information and developed curriculum to address concerns specific to inmate parents to help them maintain a positive connection with their children. The concept became a pilot course in spring 1986 and a published book, *Parenting from a Distance: Your Rights and Responsibilities*, in early 1987. (Correctional educators in Texas, Nebraska, and Pennsylvania reviewed the manuscript before it was published. A Spanish translation of the text was released in 1998.)

I liked teaching Parenting from a Distance at least as much as I disliked teaching Victim Awareness, yet they are bound by similarities. Both ask convicted felons to look beyond themselves, think about what they have done to hurt others, and choose to make amends. But the parenting program focused on positive actions incarcerated parents could take to help their children, while the victim program, it seemed to me, focused on guilt and shame.

When crimes they commit send parents to jail or prison, their children become victims. Inmate parents have a right and responsibility to explain their crime and incarceration to their children. I consider it one of the most important tasks of their distance-parenting role. They consider it the most difficult. Stories in chapter 13 show moms and dads struggling to say, "I broke a law, and prison is my consequence."

Children separated from parents create their own ideas of the truth from comments they hear when adults in their lives don't give them clear, honest answers. They develop fears and anxieties, and they need loving encouragement to go on with their lives while the incarcerated parent does time.

Preschool-age children see themselves at the center of the universe. They tend to feel responsible for the separation and worry about what will happen to them when a parent goes to prison. "What did I do bad to make him (or her) go away? Who will love me? Who will be my mommy or my daddy? Will Santa Claus still find me on Christmas Eve? Will Daddy or Mommy know me when they see me?"

Grade-school children are saddened by separation from parents and need to express those feelings, learn it's okay to cry, and learn how sad feelings lead to angry actions. In their stage of development, they are learning to think about rules and values, and they are developing internal controls.

Teens fear they will make the same mistakes their incarcerated parents made. They need help seeing themselves as individuals separate from their parents and peers. They need permission to express their feelings about prison and its impact on their lives.

All children at every age and stage of development need to know the incarcerated parent is okay. Communication with inmate parents alleviates many anxieties and fears set up by the unknown, and by movies and TV shows depicting the horrors of jail and prison. While I taught at the women's prison, an inmate's son hitchhiked from Florida to see her. Of course he was denied admittance: he wasn't on her approved visiting list. He was one of many children who set out to find a parent lost to the system.

The young son of another incarcerated woman began acting out in dangerous ways, once setting a fire at a group home. He wanted the police to put him in prison with his mother. Without communication with her, he had no understanding of the system.

Parenting from a Distance explored those truths and taught simple things: telephone etiquette, preparing for phone conversations, writing letters to children, making cassette tapes for them, celebrating birthdays and holidays from a distance, selecting TV programs children and parents could watch separately and talk or write letters about later. It taught complex things too: answering difficult questions about crimes and prison; handling financial concerns, including financial support children might expect from the incarcerated parent; preparing for reuniting and problems both children and parents encounter during those transitions; and learning about laws that affect children and families.

Students read dependency laws and codes that affect children and families and learned to cooperate with their children's primary caregivers, especially regarding visiting. In time they begged for information on realistic expectations of visits inside the fence and how children often act out afterward. Children might fuss and cry; revert to earlier developmental stages (thumb-sucking, wetting or soiling, tantrum throwing); and withdraw into sadness. That's normal. Almost all children readjusted within a day or two, but not all caregivers were willing to cope with the behavior, and some used it as a reason to avoid taking children on prison visits.

Men enrolled in Parenting from a Distance discussed conflicts they encountered with their children's mothers at visits and about coming to visit. "We have to work harder to help them understand what we're learning," one said. "We messed up; we're in prison; we've probably learned more about positive parenting and children's needs than they'll ever have time to hear. They're busy doing the hard job. They're parenting every day."

He was right: they had learned more theory than most of their children's mothers or caregivers. I reminded them that it's easier to come up with solutions for parenting struggles when the children aren't there fussing, misbehaving, and demanding immediate attention. One night an agitated student told the class he'd just had another fight with his old lady. "She's having a rough time with our son, so I was trying to give her some advice, and she hung up on me."

After his classmates commiserated, in male inmate language, I asked what advice he'd given.

"I told her she's handling him all wrong, she needs to learn a few things."

"She's mothering an eight-year-old boy by herself, and you told her she's doing it wrong?"

"Yeah, because she is."

"Let me see," I said. "What analogy can I use to span the sex differences here? I think telling a woman she's parenting wrong would be akin to telling a man he's making love wrong."

Groans followed, but they were "aha" groans. Point taken. The story, without the student's name, became part of future lectures. Teachers learn so much from students. I learned they needed more than concepts: they needed help in sharing the concepts with those involved with their children.

One part of Parenting from a Distance involved inmate moms' learning where their children lived, went to school, and played or hung out, and offering similar information about themselves. Women drew pictures of their living-unit rooms, complete with measurements from wall to wall, so children could get a mental picture of the space where their moms slept, wrote letters, listened to music, and did homework. A living-unit supervisor stormed into my classroom, paper clutched in his hand, veins bulging in his neck.

"What the hell is this?" He saw escape plans in the making. Room floor plans were not to be mailed out.

A simple floor plan that showed a bed, a desk, and a chair didn't look like an escape plan to me, but I helped the women use descriptive words to show their children their home. My students, determined women all, continued sending out floor plans. The mail-room officer didn't think they were a big deal, and the women liked drawing them. Some did elevations to scale and included the room's bulletin board, where children's pictures could be posted.

The incident reminded me to teach every parental right and responsibility with cautions attached. Students made things for their children as part of their course work, and we needed to clear them for mailing before they were created. Since we had assorted fabric and notions available at the women's prison, students made soft craft items such as small pillow covers or stuffed animals without the stuffing (since it could contain contraband), fabric books for infants and very young children, and other small items. They worked with paper to create cards, picture frames, and refrigerator art with colored paper, pens, pencils, glitter, and assorted supplies they were permitted to use on items they wished to mail out. I acquired rubber stamps, ink pads, stencils, and coloring books to help them create their art. They added talent and love.

The first time I taught Parenting from a Distance to dads, I expected them to have less interest in the lab part of the class than women showed and was shocked to find they had at least as much interest. Men not enrolled in parenting classes came begging for materials too. Those who qualified for hobby shop at MICC could get art supplies sent in if they had money to pay for them. Most didn't; they just wanted one design from a coloring book. I never learned to turn away such requests. The education office personnel groaned about all the photocopying I did, and they were right: much of it wasn't for my students, and some of it likely violated copyright laws. Precious Moments kids, Disney characters, and alphabet motifs were popular. I hope sharing a few trade-marked designs with incarcerated dads will be forgiven.

Men traced the designs onto cards they created or onto blank three-by-five puzzles I found at craft stores, then colored them with the care a fine artist gives to a canvas. One man, whose daughter refused to respond to his letters, heard she had showed off her puzzle and cards to a friend of his and bragged about her dad making them. She wasn't yet ready to write to him, but she clung to the things he sent her.

Now and then a man brought prison designs to class to share. If I deemed them inappropriate for children, they could not be used in the classroom. (Prison designs are heavy on barbed wire, roses and hearts dripping blood, heavy metal, gang graffiti, and tattoo-shop drawings.)

Men also painted with watercolors on assorted kinds of paper and left their work in the classroom to dry, so at times it was difficult to find a surface for the next class to do academic work. Teaching assistants knew those creations were valued and protected them. Preschools often hang wet work on clotheslines, but such lines weren't permitted in prison. We had to find surfaces, including the floor and desk in my office.

I kept a supply of large envelopes to send out big items, but most men made their own envelopes for cards and puzzles. They traced around patterns the teaching assistants made from file folders procured from the paper-recycling bin, and sometimes an unattended desk. Clean file folders made good card stock because felt-pen ink didn't run or bleed on them.

Creative inmates turned bits and pieces of wastebasket scraps into art objects. Foil from staff members' tossed cigarette packs (inmates had to roll their own smokes) was wrapped around paper picture frames, or woven into coasters and mats. Colored paper could be torn and arranged in collages or designs. Affirmations and sayings I distributed or wrote on the board were copied onto construction paper scraps to make bookmarks. Some went home to children or mothers; others stayed inside for personal use. As the flowers I brought to the classroom faded, men asked for them or collected those already tossed. They pressed them to send out with a letter or drew around the petals and leaves to create "the real look."

I fondly remember those men, with biceps bulging, coloring their cards and puzzles; following each other's suggestions on using glitter; separating lace doilies to make valentines for children, moms, and girlfriends; and wrapping their huge fingers around the blunt-point children's scissors I kept locked in the supply cupboard.

Men knew open door and parenting lab were privileges and protected them. Now and then I heard about altercations when supplies gone missing turned up in the wrong hands. (Carbon paper they used to transfer designs onto cards and puzzles disappeared at a rapid rate. Inmates used it for tattooing, an infractionable offense.) I didn't condone physical repercussions for lost supplies and developed a mantra: stolen items ultimately get to children; let it go. I accepted supply theft as part of teaching inside the fence, though it always upset me to open a cupboard and discover items missing. Word on the prison wireless, after an especially large loss, implicated a part-time teacher who allegedly "borrowed" from my supply cupboard for his class.

"They're doing crafts in his class?" That seemed odd.

"No, he gives things out as rewards when students do well."

I confronted the teacher, explained that the items had been purchased with my program's funds (and many by me, though I didn't always admit how much personal money I spent; it was a violation of prison rules). He said he hadn't taken anything, but he protested too much. I moved the more costly supplies, especially the highly desired puzzles, from the classroom cupboard to my office file cabinet.

A change took place within men as they created simple items for their children: an awareness of their connection to humanity, perhaps. I saw a difference, felt it like a welcome breeze, yet cannot prove it mattered. Even one of the by-the-book officers who worked on the education floor conceded as much. What did he, a trained officer, see during his frequent passes by the classroom? Men sitting around tables covered with simple arts and crafts supplies. Men intent on a project. Men helping one another. If he had listened in, as I did, he would have heard them talking with pride and love about their children. He'd have heard sorrows at hurts they'd inflicted, and joys at connections they'd made.

When I gained permission to hold open door sessions, men

came for craft projects and left with valuable academic information. We never did just crafts during those hours. Men came seeking help with a letter and left with a simple card to send a child. Often, while men worked on projects at the classroom tables, I helped individuals complete paperwork for the Office of Support Enforcement (OSE) so their children would have the legal connection needed to ensure future child support. Low-income parents (all of my students qualified) were required by law to pay a minimum twenty-five dollars per month per child. By registering with OSE, men accepted their obligation and contributed what they could toward their accruing debt. If they didn't register, the OSE could assume the parent's income was much higher. Their debt then accrued at a higher rate. Men I'd never seen, many of them non–English speaking, came to open door sessions for help with their OSE papers and letters to courts and agencies to which they'd been asked to respond. I kept standard letters on disk, typed in individual names and DOC numbers, and printed out their letters while they waited. It took only a few minutes to lift their burden of concern. Many men, even native English speakers, didn't know where to sign a business letter, so I learned to hand them a pen and point to the signature space.

Open Door complicated matters for the education floor's officers, who must know who is on the floor each hour. The added names of men who came for Open Door meant more work, especially if they stayed through period movement to eavesdrop on a lecture or get help writing to a loved one. Their names, DOC numbers, and living-unit information had to be added to each hour's class roster. I often got too busy helping men with individual needs, helping the group collectively, and watching in wonder to remember those additions.

Parenting students also had permission to record cassette tapes for their children. The institution sold tapes at inmate store and had absolute rules about what could be mailed out. Men read stories on tape, talked to their children, asked questions, and sometimes added music. One man got an angry note from his child because he asked questions, but didn't pause for her to answer. Another man's mother called me to ask if her son could record a new tape: she'd "accidentally" run over the one her nine-year-old grandson played every time they were in the car. "I couldn't stand hearing it one more time," she said, "and now I'm sorry. I didn't understand how much it meant to the boy just to hear his dad's voice."

One Open Door day, a young man sent by the education counselor to enroll in a writing class I taught whined and moaned while he waited. Some men were in the classroom working on projects for their children. I could feel them watching him. When I finished a task and turned to him, he tossed a form at me and said, "I don't needs none of you's ejication, I gots me a job on the outs, I is a hit man."

While I looked at him, eyebrow raised, the other men looked at me.

"How does your mama feel about you being a hit man?" I asked.

The man's head and arms jerked back like he'd been slugged. "What you be knowin' 'bout my mama?"

"She didn't rear you to shoot people; she's been worried sick about you for a long time now; she's relieved you're in prison because it's safer than being on those streets. She wants you to learn something in here so you can get a real job when you get out."

"How you be knowin' all that?"

"I get messages directly from my own parents who died over twenty years ago." I watched him frown. "Little messages from them come through all the time."

"How they be doin' that?"

"By what they taught me about the worth of learning and knowledge. By all they instilled in me. Education is a privilege, denied in many parts of the world. You're a lucky man: your crimes brought you to prison, where education is offered to you. All you have to do is get out of bed and go to a classroom."

The man sat down. "What you gonna make me do in this here class you be wantin' to push on me?"

"I'm not going to make you do anything. I'm going to assign

writing exercises. You may choose to do them or deal with the consequences."

He said, "Shit, man," and looked around the room for support.

One of my regulars said, "Clean up your mouth, man. We work on things for our children in this classroom, and we don't use potty words."

Statements I made in class (I called it bathroom language) often came back from a student's mouth. Luckily the student who spoke up was older, bigger, built like a linebacker, and of the same ethnicity as the hit man.

More and more men of the hit man's ilk arrived at MICC; more and more found their way to classes I taught. All my parenting and family classes had to be rewritten to reach ever-lower reading and comprehension levels, and I was assigned more basic skills courses. I taught parenting in them, too.

Through the years, students often thanked me for developing and teaching the distance-parenting concept by bringing me flowers and verse. Their flowers were drawings sketched onto whatever paper they had; their verse paeans of thanks for recognizing worth in them, increasing their understanding of children's needs, and helping them reach out to their family members. Many said I not only taught them, I also parented them.

That happens when one teaches parenting. How could it not?

23 A Day in Court

Getting subpoenaed to court also happens when one teaches parenting to inmates. I went many times, found each experience emotionally draining, and developed a lasting empathy for those caught up in the process.

When parents go to prison, arrangements must be made for the care of their children. Children whose fathers offend generally remain with their mothers. When mothers are arrested, someone other than the father almost always steps in as primary caregiver. Most often, the children's maternal grandparents or other relatives take the children into their homes. And almost all children of inmates become dependents of the state so the non-incarcerated parent or relative can receive financial assistance for the children's care.

Hundreds of inmate parents who enrolled in Parenting from a Distance had children receiving assistance from the state. If the father and mother were married, the noninmate parent was eligible for welfare monies for the children. Under current state law, unmarried incarcerated fathers must either declare their paternity or submit to state-ordered blood tests to establish paternity before the children's mothers receive assistance.

In addition to providing child support monies, dependency

status allows the state to determine custody and placement of the children. State laws require dependency decisions to be "in the best interests of the children" and to "nurture the family unit." An inmate's relatives are the state's first choice for placement, but they must meet the law's expectations for custody, control, and care. Not all relatives meet those requirements. In such cases, the children are placed in foster family homes or group-care facilities.

Children who become dependents of the state may be assigned a guardian *ad litem* or a court-appointed special advocate (CASA) volunteer to represent their interests. Such guardians act independently of other persons involved in the case, collect information from persons who know the child, and pass the data on to courts and social services agencies. They may visit incarcerated parents in prison or jail and may interview DOC personnel, including teachers, who work with the inmate parents. I spoke with many guardians *ad litem* who worked as unpaid volunteers. They cared about children and wanted a resolution in their best interests. They asked intelligent questions and they listened. (During my tenure in correctional education, I heard many inmate complaints about decision-making officials who refused to listen.)

The state has the right to seek termination of the parent-child relationship if no parent, relative, or legal guardian is available and willing to care for the child, or if the child is in clear and cogent danger in the home. Termination of the parent-child relationship makes the child eligible for legal adoption.

The very possibility of termination strikes terror in the hearts of inmate parents and sends them running to prison personnel who might help them. More inmates than I can count came to me for help; most, but not all, maintained their parental rights by showing the court that termination of those rights would not be in their children's best interests, and by explaining how they could contribute to their children's physical care and/or emotional well-being in the near future.

In my first experience with a petition to terminate the parent-child relationship case, I learned that attorneys for the state's Office of the Attorney General have little admiration for those who work with convicted offenders. It seemed to me they came to court with a decision made regarding a child or children's needs and found testimony that might interfere with their decision a nuisance, a buzzing fly to swat into silence. Several times judges banged gavels while I was on the stand and ordered an attorney to permit me to answer. When attorneys argued I was feeding the court information not requested, judges replied that they were in fact the court and did wish to hear what the witness had to say.

I'm neither maligning attorneys nor exalting judges. State attorneys who filed termination cases believed such an outcome would be in the best interests of the children. They had reviewed caseworkers' findings of the children's and parent's history and seen little hope for reuniting the family in a timely fashion. Judges must have suffered the weight of such decisions and wanted all the information they could gather, including corrections employees' assessments of the inmate parent and parent educators' understanding of children's developmental needs.

I often knew little about the children whose futures were at stake unless they had been victims of the incarcerated parent. Other evidentiary findings were confidential and not included in inmates' DOC records, which I rarely read to avoid tainting my opinion and view of the inmate as a student.

My first court appearance as an expert witness was for Judith, whose daughter, then eleven, had suffered neglect, including malnourishment in early childhood and some degree of physical abuse. The child had been placed in a group-care facility because she had "failed" in foster care. The state sought termination of parental rights of both parents so the child could be placed for adoption.

"I don't think she's adoptable," Judith's attorney said, "but I understand why the state feels compelled to terminate. The child has been bounced around. Terminating will give the state more muscle. They want her in a permanent home for disturbed children."

That's the gist of what I knew going into court. I testified to children's needs for ongoing contact with birth parents they'd lived with through their early years; stated that the court could schedule when a parent could send mail and make phone calls; agreed the child needed a primary caregiver, a role the mother could not fulfill while incarcerated; and explained specifics of children's physical, emotional, intellectual, and social development at age eleven. The state's attorney objected that much of my testimony was irrelevant; the judge, who knew it was relevant to the child, overruled her.

The attorney then badgered me about child abuse. "Do you know this child's history? Do you know what this mother has done to this child? Yes or No?"

She knew my knowledge of the child's history would be sketchy at best since Judith was not doing time for child abuse. Judith had told me there were times she had neglected to protect her daughter from the child's father. Though I kept my eyes on the attorney, I could see Judith kept her shoulders square, but let her chin fall to her chest.

The state's attorney may have been angry about the abuse the child suffered, or she may have been angry at the judge for overruling her objection, but her next question hurt her case against Judith. "Do you know this child described ejaculatory fluid to her caseworker? Do you know the child remembers ejaculatory fluid from when she was six or seven years of age? Yes or No?"

"No," I said, "but that would have to be male abuse."

"Yes or no, just answer yes or no," she shouted, while the judge hammered his gavel.

"My answer is no, I did not know." Brevity isn't one of my strengths.

Two or three weeks later, word came from Judith's counsel. The judge did not terminate her rights, but ordered the child to a state facility for psychiatric care. All correspondence would be monitored. Visiting, once Judith was released from prison, would be determined according to the child's needs and progress. Judith remained a mother, but with little chance to participate in her daughter's life. Still, it gave her hope, as important as food and water to someone doing time.

I was wiser about termination cases and better prepared for

the courtroom drama the next time a subpoena reached me. State attorneys had their job to do, and I had mine, which I saw as disseminating general information about children's needs at various stages of their development along with specific information about what the parent facing termination had accomplished in parenting and family courses. More than one attorney sneered, "It's prison, not college," or a similar comment to impugn the integrity of prison classes, but it didn't work. Defense attorneys asked me to restate my educational background, my additional certification, and the prison's academic accreditation.

The most difficult case in which I participated involved an immature mother of two girls, an infant and toddler. She had moved to Washington state from the deep South with a man not the girls' biological father. Betty Lee enrolled in parenting classes even though her crime, child abuse, denied her lab participation in Pooh's Corner preschool. A viewing window to the preschool allowed her to complete observation assignments. She whined about being "locked out," but she met the course requirements.

Betty Lee's primary counselor and her prison psychiatrist both urged me to read her records before going to court. In the middle of reading them, I dashed to a restroom and threw up. Both girls had suffered heinous sexual abuse by the man, who had mental disabilities caused by shrapnel lodged in his brain. Betty hadn't protected her children from him and was doing time for her neglect.

When her attorney called to brief me about my role in the hearing, I suggested he ask questions that would allow me to argue that Betty Lee should maintain contact through supervised annual visits and explain why I believed such contact would be in the children's best interests. They would need to hear, from her, why she hadn't protected them from the abuse. The attorney said he wouldn't touch that with a ten-foot pole.

There were six attorneys in the courtroom, one who represented Betty Lee and five who represented others: the children; their foster parents, who wanted to adopt them; the male abuser, who wanted his sentence commuted because of his war record and mental disabilities; social and health services, which would have to supervise continuing care of the girls regardless of guardianship; and the state attorney general's office. To my surprise, Betty Lee's attorney opened with a question about the children's need for ongoing contact with their mother. I answered briefly, concerned I'd misread something in his question. He rephrased; I answered; five attorneys jumped to their feet, shouting, "Objection, Your Honor," with requests my words be stricken from the record.

My heart pounded. I struggled to swallow rising bile. I knew what the children had suffered.

The judge overruled; Betty Lee's attorney asked me another question. I introduced more information about children's ages, stages, and emotional needs, and I added philosophical comments about open adoption, which didn't exist in Washington state law.

Again five attorneys were on their feet. The judge banged his gavel, issued warnings, reminded the attorneys they would all have an opportunity to question me, and asked me to continue with my answer. I left wrung out. Betty Lee's attorney followed me into the corridor, offered an apology for changing his line of questioning without warning, and escorted in his next witness. I later learned a respected child psychologist from the area had offered opinions similar to mine, thus opening the door Betty Lee's attorney needed.

The judge did not terminate her rights, though he reportedly admonished her at length for her choice of male partner and advised her to have nothing further to do with the man. He named the foster parents legal guardians of the girls, with all the rights and responsibilities of the role until the children reached legal majority, but ordered supervised visitation for Betty Lee. The state social and health services agency, in cooperation with the Department of Corrections, transported her from prison to the community where the children lived, over two hundred miles east, four times a year until her release. She planned to settle there after completing her sentence, though the children would not be returned to her.

A National Institute of Justice research document published

in 2000 said, "Little is known about the effects of a parent's incarceration on childhood development, but it is likely to be significant." Some commonly-cited research on how children cope with separation and loss indicates children are generally sad and angry, may become aggressive, and struggle with self-esteem and self-control. Significant indeed.

Judith's daughter went into a care facility where she was to remain until age eighteen. Then what? Betty Lee's daughters fared better. They were assigned guardians who wanted to provide care and love. Two of my former students who are mothers lost one child each to termination so that each foster family, caring for them since infancy, could legally adopt. Both women had other children with whom they'd bonded and attached prior to committing their crimes. Both resumed care of those children. Both sets of adoptive parents permitted the birth mothers to stay in touch with their "lost" child.

One young woman who left her infant with a baby-sitter and went on a crime spree lost parental rights before the child reached eighteen months of age. Most cases aren't even filed until the child is that age; someone intervened for the foster parents, who wanted to adopt. The inmate's primary counselor said, "The child's better off." Perhaps, but the child still needs information about her birth parents, and the best persons to supply such information are the birth parents themselves.

To the officer who typed "parienting" on my MICC badge and declared prison the best thing for those men's children, and to all the prison personnel and taxpayers who ever said parents should have thought about their children before committing their crimes, I say we need to think about the children now. Emotional hurts have many layers. Children may fare well enough, and in some cases far better, with the caregivers seeing to them during their parents' imprisonment, but the reality of prison remains lodged in their awareness, their psyches.

There, again, is the reason I believe parent education should be provided to all inmates, including juvenile inmates who are also parents. Many of them need to grow up and learn to accept

responsibilities. Understanding, responsible inmate parents ultimately ease the reality for children and the burden for judges who
must decide what is in their best interests. Inmate parents have a
responsibility to their children to cooperate with the courts so the
children can be placed in safe and secure environments.

That brings me to one last story about termination, the last
time I went out to court. (I did testify two more times, by telephone connection from the courtroom.) John enrolled in parenting classes when he was returned to McNeil Island for a work-
release violation. He was angry and belligerent, and he wanted to
make me his enemy by comparing his tough life as a black male to
my easy one as a white female. John needed to show the state a
satisfactory completion of a parenting course. He was in class by
court mandate at a time when my patience had been consumed.
He needed me more than I needed him, but he refused to acknowledge that until the state filed for termination of his parent-
child relationship to free his son for adoption.

When John first went to prison, his mother took his son into
her home. The boy's mother, a drug abuser on the run from the
law, had abandoned him shortly after his birth. While John was at
work release in Seattle, his family left a car close enough to his job
so he could drive to his mother's home to visit his son. He fit it
into his schedule and didn't get caught. Father and son grew in
their attachment. It worked right up to the time John's mother
died of a heart attack and the state stepped in.

"The state snatched my son from my people and put him in a
foster home with Caucasian parents," John said. He made Caucasian into a dirty word. "I went crazy, got terminated, got sent back
inside, to this here island."

I explained how child dependency laws worked. When John's
mother, an approved foster-care provider, died, the child had to
be moved to another approved home. A member of John's family
who wanted to keep the boy didn't qualify. Unfortunately, the
state often has too few African American foster families.

Once John decided to learn parenting concepts, he aced three
separate classes, not because he was bright (which he was), but

because he loved his son. I helped him write letters to his son's caseworker and to the court, a big step for him.

"I'll help you, but I won't write for you," I said, and asked him what he'd learned.

"That I'm responsible for most of my son's problems." His son was acting out, running away from foster care, and using abusive language. John wrote, in part, "I have learned those behaviors occur when a child is angry and hurt, and he is likely angry at me and his mom. I believe I am the person who can best help him cope with his problems and feelings. At age eight, I know he would be difficult to place for adoption."

In the letter, John admitted he had sold drugs, stated he had completed a chemical dependency program, and listed the vocational certificates and college credits he had earned.

The state's attorneys couldn't attack John's performance or grades, so they dwelled on his attitude. I described it as cocky in the beginning, but dedicated once we agreed which of us was the teacher. They asked if I knew about his blatant violation of work-release rules and permitted only a yes or no answer. Before dismissing me, the judge asked if I had any further comments. He must have seen comments trying to jump out of my mouth.

"I don't approve of inmates on work release violating rules, even when the rules impede personal growth, and I told John as much. He acknowledged it was a poor choice, but said he wanted to spend time with his son and swore to me he will keep the boy out of crime and in school right on through college."

John's parental rights were not terminated. He liked to say he won his case. I like to think his son won, and so did society. In addition, he was granted a ten-day early release. The last time I heard, father and son were making it in the real world. John's day in court worked in the best interests of his child.

24 Going Back Out

In the mid-1990s, Washington state legislators began tightening laws governing the Department of Corrections. Their actions were influenced by the same heinous crimes that inspired Project Social Responsibility, and they had a powerful leader in their ranks. State Representative Ida Ballasiotes, whose daughter was raped and murdered by a man who walked away from work release in Seattle in 1988, was elected to the House in 1992 and became the chair of the House Corrections Committee. She brought determination, and I fear a lingering anger, to her legislative work. While tough-on-crime legislation, designed to take away inmate privileges, was in debate, I wrote her and other legislators letters stating my concerns about cuts in education.

Though most of my letters went unanswered, I did hear from two influential people. Representative Clyde Ballard, Speaker of the House at that time, responded with thanks, as did then secretary of the Department of Corrections Chase Riveland, who I knew questioned the wisdom of such legislation. As a corrections consultant to the National Institute of Corrections, Riveland now advocates for programs to help inmates learn to help themselves.

Media coverage of changing legislation focused heavily on taking away inmates' privileges, especially television in their rooms or cells and weight lifting. Though news reporters mentioned changes in educational privileges, especially the elimination of college-level courses, most of the footage showed images of lazy inmates watching daytime TV and buffed-up prisoners getting out to offend again.

The enacted legislation denies inmates' personal possession of a television set for at least sixty days following completion of intake and evaluation. It prohibits inmates convicted of aggravated assault from participating in weight lifting for a period of two years, and it empowers superintendents to further prohibit such activity if the inmate is determined by correctional evaluation to be a threat to others.

I consider both decisions reasonable.

It also requires all inmates to participate in department-approved education or work programs, or both, unless they are medically unable. That too is reasonable.

My concern then and now focuses on educational opportunities and expectations for inmates. Those who test below eighth-grade level are expected to take part in Adult Basic Education, which they need. But if we truly want them to succeed, they also need much more: vocational training that fits business and industry requisites, and a commitment from employers to hire former felons; life skills training that includes parenting and family education, chemical dependency treatment and education, anger management, and job-search preparation; and other personal training that will help them cope outside the fence. Over the years, many inmates who returned to prison after being released spoke to me about being overwhelmed by bus schedules, getting and following directions in areas unknown to them, job applications, grocery shopping, and family members who didn't understand their fears of such everyday matters.

The legislature adopted a plan to reduce the per-pupil cost of instruction by incorporating more volunteers and more technology. The system is making some progress with computer-based learning, though inmates misuse computers and administrators remove them from classrooms. Then what?

Many churches provide spiritual outreach to inmates. To my knowledge, every religion is represented with programs inside the fence, as are social programs such as Alcoholics Anonymous. The women's prison has many volunteers with many talents and skills, but few go inside to provide academic assistance. The men's prisons have attracted fewer volunteers per capita, but they depend on those who go inside to supplement DOC funded programs.

When I left McNeil Island in mid-1997, the legislature's expectation was for volunteers to provide parent education. That has not happened. The classes I taught no longer exist. Superintendent Alice Payne and her staff do sponsor annual family events that encourage parent-child attachment. The women's prison does the same. The events are paid for with inmate funds.

I continued teaching through the early years of the prison education changes and worked hard to comply with legislative and taxpayer expectations. Prior to the cutbacks, I taught Chemical Dependency and Family Issues for college social services/mental health credit. Many inmate students completed the class with outstanding performances and an awakened understanding of the impact their addictions had on family members.

I also taught Parenting From a Distance; Positive Parenting, which introduced basic concepts of child rearing; Behavior Management, which focused on problem solving for individuals and parents; Coping with Separation, which taught inmates how children handle the separation and grief of a parent's incarceration; and Family History and Patterns, designed to help students examine how family and culture influence identity, values, attitudes, self-concept, and decision making.

After the education changes, I taught all the same concepts, with different course numbers and titles. I rewrote almost all the material so it could be read and understood by inmates in Adult Basic Education. I continued teaching writing courses, and I was expected to emphasize writing in every class. No problem there; I'd always encouraged writing.

Department of Corrections–sponsored chemical dependency programs are available inside prisons. Thus, the need for classes

through the education department were questioned. Programs offered by DOC were facilitated by men or women in recovery.
They'd walked the walk and they talked the talk, unlike me. I completed the same training as those facilitators, but I wasn't even an
adult child of alcoholics, so my expertise was questioned. What
I brought to the program was extensive training in and a clear
understanding of developmental ages and stages. Addiction inter-
feres with development, especially emotional development. Most
recovered addicts who ran programs had missed huge chunks of
their adolescence and young adulthood; many started using so
young that it affected their preadolescence.

I also had inmates' respect, and I was asked many times to
continue teaching chemical dependency classes. The first quarter
after the college course was eliminated, I offered similar material
as a noncredit substance abuse class. Thirty-four students enrolled, many of them ESL (English as a Second Language) students. The education director divided the class into two sections
and rounded up volunteer TAs to help. They had to register as
students to get into my classroom. I spent my off-hours at the
computer rewriting curriculum to include bullet statements and
plenty of white space. I may not have walked the walk, but I
walked miles in the classroom, talking to each man, helping with
comprehension.

I went from full-time employment to three-quarters time,
three afternoons and three nights a week, to avoid a difficult morning commute and to spend mornings developing basic skills–level
materials.

I started burning out. More students with attitudes similar to
the hit man's ("I don't needs none of you's ejication . . .") enrolled
in my classes. Too many wanted the letter of completion I wrote
for every student in every class without doing the work to earn it.
Several young black men required to take part in education because of their low test scores wanted me, the system, and all of
society to give them what had been taken from them all these
years by whites. Those who irritated me most were light-skinned
sons of white mothers and black fathers. They discounted the

worth of their mothers, who reared them, and elevated the worth of their fathers, who had long since abandoned them.

When more mature black students told me to give up on the punks, whether they be African American, Hispanic, Asian, or Caucasian, I listened. Those men had come from the streets too, and they had made a personal commitment to learn and change while inside the fence so that they could live when they got out. I made Choosing to Change a writing and discussion assignment in every class, and I was schooled by the pros—the inmates who would make it outside the fence. Men of all ethnic backgrounds, men who had lived under bridges and survived on food found in dumpsters, men who had committed serious crimes, and men who had committed long strings of minor felonies all said the same thing, something I'd always known: even the best teachers can't teach those who refuse to learn.

After tendering my resignation, I wrote a manual, "We're Still Members of the Family: Curriculum for ABE Students in Prison Classrooms," for Adult Basic Education teachers to use with their students. It covers child development, parenting, and family history and patterns. I used it in an all-day workshop with my colleagues at MICC and gave them copies as a farewell gift. For me it represented the end of one stage of my life, the closing of one door and the opening of another.

A writer friend suggested I submit the manual for publication. I queried the American Correctional Association. Though they were interested, the additional work I would need to do to make it usable for students below fourth-grade level seemed daunting. I tossed it in the drawer and wrote fiction drawn from my child and family studies training and background until I could no longer ignore the need to write nonfiction. I then began writing this account of my correctional education career.

In 2003, legislators in Washington—the first state to pass a "three stikes" law—began rethinking their costly sentencing policies. One law passed during the session will shorten sentences for drug offenders and provide money for drug treatment. Another will increase earned time toward earlier release for inmates convicted of drug and property crimes. A newspaper article reports about twenty-five states have passed similar laws. After two decades that saw prison building boom and sentence time increase while education and other program budgets were cuts, change is again in the wind.

In his book *Going Up the River: Travels in a Prison Nation*, Pulitzer Prize–winning journalist Joseph T. Hallinan argues that incarceration is big business—in fact, an industrial complex. Prisons provide jobs to citizens in the communities where they're built.

Consider the statistics. American taxpayers spend thirty billion dollars per year to house nearly two million offenders in federal and state prisons and local jails, and untold millions more to prosecute an increasing number of offenders who will push costs and inmate numbers ever higher. At the same time, our nation's families, communities, and cities are annually reabsorbing some six hundred thousand offenders who leave prison much as they entered.

Currently 1 in every 109 American men, including nearly 10 percent of black males age twenty-five to twenty-nine, and 1 in every 1,695 American women are in prison or jail. Prisons must prepare them to rejoin us in our homes, workplaces, and communities, not merely warehouse them until their sentences are served.

In the first chapter of this book, I asked if my eighteen-year career mattered. In 1998 the Washington Correctional Education Association gave me their Apple Award for outstanding contribution to the WCEA and to correctional education. It had been awarded only once before, in 1995. Pierce College honored me with a Dean's Award for Outstanding Service, Tacoma Community College with an Award of Appreciation for Dedicated Compassion for Students.

Those awards came from within professional ranks, and though I appreciate them, I believe the most important measure of my work is represented by some of the stories in this book that show inmates working to learn and change and to reach out to their families. There are many more stories I'd like to tell, but I will close with one that is particularly meaningful to me because it involves an inmate's family member. About two years after leaving correctional education, I borrowed some wallpaper books from a Tacoma retail outlet. The woman helping me asked my name for her records.

"Jan Walker?" she said. "That name sounds so familiar."

We discussed and dismissed the various ways we might have met. Finally, I asked if she worked at McNeil Island between 1990 and 1997. Her head turned away. She looked down at the desk where we stood. Then she looked back at me, and though we talked for some time, I wish to share only one part of our conversation.

"That's how I know your name. My husband was one of your parenting students. It helped us," she said. "It helped a lot."